AF266983

RUMOR

ART

ESSAYS

VILÉM FLUSSER

METAFLUX // VILÉM FLUSSER

§ The philosopher Vilém Flusser was born in Prague in 1920 but emigrated to Brazil, fleeing Nazi persecution at the outbreak of war in 1939. After a short stay in London, he arrived in Rio de Janeiro with his wife and parents-in-law at the end of 1940. The Flussers settled in São Paulo, where they lived for thirty-two years. In the early 1970s they moved back to Europe, settling first in Italy and then in Robion, France, where they lived until Vilém Flusser's untimely death in a car crash in 1991, after leaving a symposium in Prague.
§ While living in Brazil, Flusser wrote for Brazilian periodicals and taught at several academic institutions, including the University of São Paulo, the Brazilian Institute of Philosophy, and the Institute of Technology and Aeronautics. His first two books, *Language and Reality* and *The History of the Devil*, were published in Brazil during the 1960s. In the late 1970s and 1980s Flusser travelled throughout Europe, lecturing and participating in conferences and symposia and publishing his best-known titles. He came to prominence in the field of media philosophy after publishing his seminal book *Towards a Philosophy of Photography* in 1983, which was followed shortly by *Into the Universe of Technical Images* in 1985 and *Does Writing Have a Future?* in 1987. § A polyglot, Flusser wrote in four languages: German, Portuguese, English, and French. The "Metaflux//Vilém Flusser" collection aims to present high quality translations of Flusser's Brazilian writings to an international readership. These include his academic courses, monographs, essays, and letters, as well as works originally written in English.
§ The "Metaflux//Vilém Flusser" collection is possible due to the generous support of Miguel Gustavo Flusser.

ARTFORUM // ESSAYS

1. Communication Theory;
2. Philosophy; 3. Art

First edition ©2017 Metaflux Publishing
Series Editor Rodrigo Maltez Novaes
Editor Martha Schwendener
Editorial Assistant Candice Chu
Design by Chagrin
Published by Metaflux Publishing
www.metafluxpublishing.com

ISBN 978 0 9933272 3 0

Apparatus Homini Lupus

V. Flusser, 1983

Metaflux 2017

INTRODUCTION

§ Vilém Flusser was excited to be writing for *Artforum.* He had never heard of the magazine before being asked to contribute to its pages, but he had published hundreds of essays in journals and newspapers in Europe and Brazil. In the 1960s and 1970s he had his own columns in *O Estado de São Paulo* and *Folha de São Paulo,* two of Brazil's biggest newspapers. Later he wrote for German newspapers and for *European Photography* magazine. He was thrilled, however, at the prospect of his work appearing regularly in an English-language publication. § The first of his twenty "Curie's Children" essays was published in the September 1986 issue of *Artforum* alongside Max Kozloff's review of the English translation of Umberto Eco's *Travels in Hyperreality*; artist Barbara Kruger's column on television; Carol Squiers writing on photojournalism; Frederic Tuten's micro-fiction about a young artist named Rex; Greil Marcus musing on Cold War pulp magazines; Glenn O'Brien on televised talent shows; and Lisa Liebmann on the phenomenon of cigar-smoking celebrities. It was an explosion of cross-disciplinary cultural criticism. § Flusser's essay, "On Science," appeared at the end of this section. His column feels different from that of the other writers: less obsessed with pop culture; clearly less American. But it fit into *Artforum*'s mid-eighties mission to expand its coverage and the field of visual art. Into seven paragraphs, Flusser packed a dense meditation on light, from Enlightenment reason and artificial intelligence to technology after Auschwitz, Hiroshima, and Chernobyl. The essay bridges media theory, digitisation and biotechnology, but it is primarily philosophical, arguing that we are on the cusp of a new form of cognition, a new age in which knowledge will move between brain synapses and semiconductors. "Postmodernism is this conundrum of oscillation," Flusser concluded. § Flusser's path to *Artforum* was — to use one of his favorite terms — *nomadic*. Born in Prague in 1920, he studied philosophy at Charles University for two semesters until the Nazi occupation in 1939 ended his formal education. Fleeing to London with his

Martha Schwendener

future wife, Edith Barth, and her family, the group finally landed in Brazil in 1940. Flusser's father, the director of a technical academy in Prague and a champion of the first Czechoslovak Republic, had been offered a position at Jerusalem University, which he declined. Instead he remained in Prague with Flusser's mother, sister and grandparents — all of whom perished in Nazi concentration camps. Auschwitz would become a central motif in Flusser's writing: the logical outcome of Western rationality rather than an aberration; the prototypical Enlightenment apparatus.

§ The Flussers spent thirty-two years in Brazil, coinciding with that country's attempt at accelerated development ("50 Years in Five" was the motto of the Kubitschek presidency in the 1950s), the 1964 military coup, and subsequent dictatorship. During the forties and fifties Flusser worked for his father-in-law in an import-export business, and later started his own company manufacturing radios and transistors, and doing "philosophy at night," which meant reading a broad variety of texts. Because of his forced migration, he never earned a college degree, which plagued him for most of his life. Even after becoming a successful journalist, publishing in Brazilian philosophy journals, books in Portuguese and French, and teaching at institutions in São Paulo and France, he would write to North American universities asking if he might obtain employment. The answer was usually "no." § And so Flusser entered the art world. His circle of friends in São Paulo included the artists Samson Flexor and Mira Schendel, both Jewish refugees from Europe. In 1964 he was appointed to the advisory board of the São Paulo Bienal, for which he served briefly as Technical Director. In 1972, at the General Assembly of the International Association of Art Critics (AICA) in Paris, Flusser presented a radical proposal for restructuring the Bienal around a networked, communications model.[1] He described his idea in prescient terms as a "laboratory" for art and communication rather than a platform for nations to present their best artists. However, an ongoing boycott of the São Paulo Bienal, protesting the military dictatorship, haunted the proceedings.

North American artists like Gordon Matta-Clark and Hans Haacke had been involved in the 1969 boycott and persuaded György Kepes, director of the Center for Advanced Visual Studies at the Massachusetts Institute of Technology, who had organised an art and technology exhibition for the Bienal, to withdraw. Delegates in Paris proposed extending the boycott through 1973 — or until the dictatorship ended. Flusser took an opposing view: easy to protest from an armchair in Paris, he argued; harder if you were a Brazilian artist who could not leave the country. (Schendel did participate in the 1973 Bienal, mounting an installation that read as a thinly veiled protest-prayer.)
§ Flusser would remain in contact with a number of figures he met during this period, including René Berger; Louis Bec, who illustrated Flusser's parabiological fable *Vampyroteuthis infernalis* (1987); the video artist Fred Forest; and Abraham A. Moles, who was among the first to apply information theory to aesthetics. In 1972, the Flussers moved to Merano, a spa town in Northern Italy where Franz Kafka, one of Flusser's primary inspirations — particularly

as a Prague Jew writing in German — once spent a few months hoping to cure his tuberculosis. Hiking in the mountains of the South Tyrol, Flusser began to think about "the nature-culture problem." The resulting book was *Natural:Mind*, a collection of essays published in Portuguese in 1979 that set out to destroy the nature-culture dialectic and serve as a European "tourist guide" for Brazilians. ("'Tourist guide,'" Flusser wrote, "as long as 'tourism' is understood as an updated synonym of the term 'theory.'")[2] § The Flussers finally settled in Robion, an unspectacular village in Provence, compared to its more famous neighbours. Flusser taught in local art schools and universities and participated in conferences in Avignon, Aix-en-Provence, and Arles and continued to write in the short form, following the example of Ortega y Gasset, whose books were composed of essays originally published in newspapers or delivered as lectures. The resulting books, *The Power of the Everyday* (1973), *The Codified World* (1974), *Post-History* (1983), and *Gestures* (1991) reflect Flusser's interest in objects, language, phenomenology, communications and mass media. Flusser's U.S. exposure remained limited, although he delivered the paper "Two Approaches to the Phenomenon, Television" at "Open Circuits: The Future of Television," a 1974 conference at the Museum of Modern Art in New York organised by Electronic Arts Intermix and Gerald O'Grady of the Center for Media Study at the State University of New York at Buffalo.[3] § A turning point came in 1981, when Flusser met Andreas Müller-Pohle, an artist who also published and edited *European Photography* magazine. Müller-Pohle encouraged Flusser to write the essays for *Towards a Philosophy of Photography* (1983), which became the first book in his technical image trilogy, followed by *Into the Universe of Technical Images* (1985) and *Does Writing Have a Future?* (1987). Technical images include photography, but also film, television, satellite, and computer-generated images — as well as holograms, one of Flusser's favorite formats, and which were popular in the seventies and eighties. Following thinkers like Bertolt Brecht, Michel Foucault, and Giorgio Agamben, Flusser was more interested in the apparatus of the camera rather than individual images. (Unlike Roland Barthes' *Camera Lucida*, there are no images reproduced in *Towards a Philosophy of Photography*.) For Flusser, the camera was the prototypical post-historical apparatus, a black box whose program was codified by its programmers and performed by its functionaries, the same way Adolf Eichmann served as a functionary for the Nazi apparatus. But it could be challenged by artists or others who work against the program. *Into the Universe of Technical Images* and *Does Writing Have a Future?* consider the philosophical ramifications: how images made from "particles" affect human cognition and history. If written and spoken language were no longer capable of conveying meaning and the concept of linear history was dissolved, artists, critics and philosophers would be in the vanguard of shaping this new world. § Flusser's technical image writings resulted in new collaborations and correspondences with artists and theorists like Harun Farocki, Joan Foncuberta, and Friedrich Kittler. He remained relatively unknown in North

America, however. One person who was aware of Flusser was Max Kozloff, a writer and photographer who had been involved with *Artforum* since the sixties. Kozloff met Flusser at a 1982 colloquium at the International Center for Photography in New York and they carried on a friendly correspondence. In 1986, Kozloff sent an essay of Flusser's to *Artforum*. He wrote to Flusser:

§ *This journal is the one with which I have been associated for many years; I gave you a copy with my piece on narrative photography. It is now a restless art magazine, with a lot of input of the wrong (jargonistic) kind from Europe, where it is widely read. Here, it is almost getting to look like the "Rolling Stones" of the art world, so you should have a piquant context. [Ingrid Sischy] sounded as if she might be eager for more.*[4]

§ It was a good time to be arriving at *Artforum*. Founded in 1962 in San Francisco, the magazine moved to New York in 1966 and quickly became an important organ for criticism of non-traditional art media and a proving ground for a new breed of academically trained critics. In 1979, Ingrid

Sischy was appointed editor at the age of twenty-seven. Her tenure coincided with the rise of the East Village and a robust market for painting. She was credited with bringing film, fashion, architecture, television and popular music into the magazine, as well as art from Europe and the global south. Photography was on Sischy's agenda, too: she had interned at the Museum of Modern Art in New York under John Szarkowski, and photography was becoming the reigning modality for art in the eighties. § Sischy was more excited about the French philosophers she had recruited to *Artforum,* such as Baudrillard, Lyotard, and Deleuze, but she and Flusser shared a similar perspective on writing. "Looking back," she commented in 2012, "I think we had an intuitive sense that the end of print was on the horizon, with the coming of computers, new technology, etc."[5] Flusser sent more essays to *Artforum* until Charles Miller, the new managing editor, wrote him in October 1986: "We now have four of your manuscripts on file, and while I don't want to dampen your enthusiasm for *Artforum,* I wanted to tell you that it may be some time until all are printed."[6] § Undeterred, and clearly hoping he had found a North American version of Müller-Pohle, Flusser wrote back to Miller explaining his position. In his writing, he had considered our "present crisis" from a variety of angles: science, history, technology, aesthetics, and digital codes. Now he was ready to synthesise these ideas, and "it so happens that our contact coincides with this turning point in my writing. This is very important for me," Flusser wrote. "Not only does our contact suggest to me that I might have found an editor who 'controls' me, but it also opens up for me the American stage, with which I had so far almost no relation."[7] Müller-Pohle was "an excellent thinker and friend," but Flusser felt he had taken up "too much of his thinking," and his Brazilian editor was "too much under my influence to be really critical of my writings." What was really important, however, was that *Artforum* was a U.S. journal since, "I know, of course, that America is the most important place to publish, because it is where most new ideas are born."[8] § And yet, Miller would not become Flusser's editor. Instead, David

Frankel, *Artforum*'s senior editor, received the essays via fax and edited them with Flusser over the phone in Robion.[9] The writing arrived in rather rough shape; English was not Flusser's best language. Frankel pieced the essays together, although neither he nor anyone else at *Artforum* was familiar with Flusser's *oeuvre*.[10] And it was an ambitious prospect, boiling an entire philosophical project down to a series of columns in an art magazine. But Flusser's key ideas shine through. § "On Communication" (*Artforum* January 1987) argues that the programmed codes of digital media lead to a new era of post-history. The "On Discovery" series, published from 1987 to 1989, explores the overlap between digital media and genetic engineering. "On Discovery V" (June 1988), a quasi-satiric essay, suggests that cows are biological machines which could eventually take over the planet — a Kafkaesque, eco-redux of the robot revolution depicted in postwar movies and science fiction. In "On Future Architecture" (April 1989) and "On An Unspeakable Future" (March 1990), homes have become perforated like Swiss cheese by cables, wires, and

Martha Schwendener

antennae,[11] and function as knots or nodes in a human network.[12] "Wondering About Science" (June 1989) looks at how post-Enlightenment philosophy and science have impacted our concept of wonder, while "On Popes" (October 1990) argues that art critics and pontiffs use words to build bridges between images and faith, a relationship that will be altered by artificial intelligence.[13] "On Three Times" (February 1991) looks at different notions of time, affected by accident and entropy. "On Three Spaces" (May 1991) considers real, virtual, and cosmic space, and "On Books" (November 1991) argues that, in the future, letters will be transcoded into images and paper books will disappear. § The *Artforum* editors were astute in connecting Flusser's ideas with other thinkers. In 1990, Frankel sent Flusser a copy of Avital Ronell's *The Telephone Book,* asking him to review it for the magazine. Flusser responded enthusiastically since he felt the book echoed "my friend Friedrich Kittler's ideas."[14] (Later, Flusser found Ronell "hard to swallow" and asked for an extension until Spring 1992).[15] But Flusser and *Artforum* were not always a perfect fit. Early on, he expressed his concerns to Miller:

§ *You are doing an excellent job and I thank you for it. There is, however, the following point we have to discuss in the future: You will have noticed that everything I write has an ironic twist to it. This is eliminated by your reformulation. I understand that this has to do with your general editing policy, but still: we must talk about this in detail.*[16]

§ Furthermore, the images used to illustrate "Curie's Children" often reflected the interests of the New York art world more than Flusser's ideas.[17] (For this collection we have chosen images that show how, in theory if not always in practice, *Artforum* was an ideal venue for his ideas.) "Curie's Children" diverged from *Artforum* in other ways. The AIDS crisis, the so-called Culture Wars, battles over reproductive rights, and the Gulf War were impacting an art world already focused on identity, authorship and the role of the artist in a hyper-capitalised society. Essays and opinion pages by Cornel West, Trinh T. Minh-ha, Kellie Jones, and Hilton Als addressing race and identity began to appear more frequently. In the September 1989 issue, Anthony Korner and Ida Panicelli, *Artforum*'s publisher and its new editor, wrote a letter expressing their concerns over cuts to the National Endowment for the Arts, describing the initiative to block the federal financing of "obscene and indecent" art as a strategy to limit what we see and think.[18] In September 1991 Panicelli asked a broader question:

§ *Is there life after postmodernism? We sense that a new discourse is in the making. But responding to the vast body of information and ideas now emerging about non-European-derived cultures, and about subjects that until recently had little or no access to the so-called mainstream of art, is a difficult task. It demands that we question not only the dichotomies of center and periphery, coloniser and colonised, but finally identity itself.*[19]

§ Flusser had addressed these concerns, but mostly in other places. That same year he published *Freedom of the Migrant: Arguments Against Nationalism* and wrote about the role of television in the December 1989 Romanian revolution, an event narrated via technical images in Harun Farocki's film "Videograms of a Revolution" (1992). Moreover, *Artforum* and the New York art world tended to favor the catastrophic view of history and politics offered by French thinkers like Baudrillard and Virilio, or the futility and ennui of a new generation of Slackers "trained on the mundane."[20] Then, on November 27, 1991, two days after delivering a lecture at the Goethe Institute in Prague – the first official lecture given in his city of birth – Flusser was killed in a car accident near the Czech-German border. *Artforum* published a brief note with his next column:

§ *It was with great sadness that the editors of Artforum heard recently of the death of Vilém Flusser, a distinguished writer and teacher of communications and a regular contributor to these pages. A number of Professor Flusser's columns for Artforum, completed but unpublished at the time of his death, will appear in the magazine in future issues.*[21]

§ "On the Term Design" was published in March 1992 in an issue devoted to commodity fetishism that also included

W.J.T. Mitchell's "The Pictorial Turn," which responded to Jonathan Crary's recently published book *Techniques of the Observer*.[22] One more essay by Flusser appeared: "On Progress" (Summer 1992), which argued that cameras, with their "phenomenological vision," are better models for progress than computers.
§ For this volume we have included eight additional essays Flusser wrote for *Artforum*, or which he revised or translated from essays he published elsewhere. "About Levers" and "Backlash" stem from Flusser's design writings, published in English as *The Shape of Things: A Philosophy of Design* (1999). For Flusser, tools mimic the human body, but with a duplicitous twist. The lever, which simulates the motions of hand and arm, "cheats" gravity. Now, however, we are in a new era in which tools like nuclear weapons and computers demand different treatment.[23] "An Improbable Story" looks at writing and the demise of books, while "Bibliophagus Convictus" uses the parabiological method Flusser devised for *Vampyroteuthis infernalis* to imagine a new species of insect that eats

only books. The last three essays, "Why Make Children," "On Branches and Sticks, Or, What is Freedom Good For?" and "On Being Subject to Objects" seem like playful musings on procreation and objects, but they are actually trapdoors into ruminating on humanity in the age of information, biotechnology, and automation. The human, Flusser writes, "is no longer a subject in any meaningful sense of the term," as we program robots to interface with the world and move closer to artificial reproduction. And yet, we still have words like "art" and "freedom," and Flusser directs his attention towards these, examining their purpose and meaning.

§ The reader will notice the similarities in the penultimate and ultimate essays. We have included both to show how Flusser wrote and continually revised his essays, often translating them into second and third languages and "turning around" his ideas, the same way a human "turns" a branch in the forest to create a more aesthetically pleasing or technologically superior stick. Flusser believed (in true postmodernist fashion) that meaning was not created in writing, but in translation, and this might be extended to his writing process, too. If Roland Barthes' "Death of the Author" resulted in the birth of the reader, and Derrida argued that meaning is deferred, for Flusser the text is an unstable entity which will one day be translated into even better languages such as technical images and computer code. § "On Progress" appeared in Ida Panicelli's last issue, before Jack Bankowsky took over as editor. Like Sischy, Bankowsky's mission dovetailed with Flusser's in uncanny ways. Bankowsky wrote in his first editor's note that the glossy art magazine is "an odd hybrid, neither scholarly journal nor trade or general-interest publication."[24] Flusser was an odd hybrid, too: a product of Central Europe and the Americas; an autodidact and philosopher whose writings were neither scholarly nor general interest, *per se*. Doing away with citations and bibliographies early in his career lodged him in that netherworld called "theory" — or what the art historian and early *Artforum* critic Rosalind Krauss has called "paraliterature." Nonetheless, Flusser's ideas had a huge impact on

European scholarship within the fields of photography theory and media studies, particularly in Germany. And his ideas were gaining hold in North America at the time of his death: the artist Jordan Crandall included Flusser's essay "In the Reservoir of Images: Photography and History" in *Blast,* an early nineties box-kit-journal that replaced the book format, and Flusser was scheduled to appear in 1992 at a Dia Center for the Arts symposium organised by the artists Gretchen Bender and Timothy Druckrey. § So why read Flusser now? Because his sometimes radical or improbable ideas about images, surfaces, bodies, and communicating through screens have turned out to be strikingly prescient. Because the connections one now sees with other strains of thought, from Judith Butler's feminist phenomenology to Felix Guattari's writings on ecology to the techno-feminism and posthumanism of Donna Haraway, N. Katherine Hayles, and Rosi Braidotti, as well as his focus on apparatus and intersubjective relations feel vital at this moment. Flusser's writings were always adopted and championed by artists first, and that has continued to be the case. His texts have been circulating at a greater rate in the U.S. art world for the last half decade and appearing in many new anthologies, coinciding with renewed interest in other thinkers from the eighties. It is a great pleasure, then — and particularly as an *Artforum* writer myself and, curiously enough, its first Internet critic — to participate in the dissemination of Flusser's ideas in English. Hopefully this book, in both words and images, will contribute to Flusser's visionary legacy.

Martha Schwendener, 2017

    Endnotes:

1. In one of the many uncanny coincidences I've encountered
    since I began working on Flusser – including our common
    publication in *Artforum* – I am on the Board of the U.S. chapter
    of AICA.

2. Vilém Flusser, *Natural:Mind*, trans. Rodrigo Maltez Novaes
    (Minneapolis: Univocal, 2013), 143.

3. Vilém Flusser, "Two Approaches to the Phenomenon,
    Television," trans. Ursula Beiter, *The New Television: A Public/
    Private Art. Essays, Statements, and Videotapes Based on "Open Circuits:
    An International Conference on the Future of Television" Organised by
    Fred Barzyk, Douglas Davis, Gerald O'Grady, and Willard Van Dyke for
    the Museum of Modern Art New York City*, ed. Douglas Davis and
    Allison Simmons (Cambridge, MA and London: MIT Press,
    1977),
    234-247.

4. Letter from Max Kozloff to Vilém Flusser, April 23, 1986,
    Vilém Flusser Archive, Berlin. In a letter the next month Kozloff
    wrote about *Artforum*, "Aside from art criticism, they have
    broad cultural interests which I think your work will excite.
    The magazine is flagrantly tied in with the commercial, trans-
    Atlantic art market, but their readership may have advantages
    for you, since it is somewhat literate but also has a respect for
    images. Do send the editor, Ingrid Sischy, other papers you
    think might be appropriate." Letter from Max Kozloff to Vilém
    Flusser, May 27, 1986, Vilém Flusser Archive, Berlin.

5. Ingrid Sischy, Interview with Michelle Kuo, *Artforum* (September
    2012): 249. Flusser even published the last book in the
    technical image trilogy, *Does Writing Have a Future?* (1987) on
    floppy disk – which meant the second edition, issued in paper-
    book form, was a kind of "failure" – although in Flusser's
    words, "not a complete failure," since it signaled the vitality of
    these ideas. Vilém Flusser, "Afterword to the Second Edition,"
    Does Writing Have a Future?, trans. Nancy Ann Roth (Minneapolis:
    University of Minnesota Press, 2011), 164.

Martha Schwendener

6.   Letter from Charles Miller to Vilém Flusser, October 9, 1986, Vilém Flusser Archive, Berlin.

7.   Letter from Vilém Flusser to Charles Miller, December 1, 1986, Vilém Flusser Archive, Berlin.

8.   Ibid.

9.   Flusser did not come up with the title for the column, although he did not challenge it. In a letter to Charles Miller, then the new Managing Editor of *Artforum*, Flusser wrote, "On my return from Brazil I find your issue containing my contribution on Light Metaphors (which you called 'Curie's Children'). I should like to express my thanks for the prompt and efficient way in which you handled the matter. It is indeed a pleasure and an honor to be collaborating with your excellent publication." Vilém Flusser letter to Charles Miller, September 1, 1986, Vilém Flusser Archive.

10. Telephone interview with David Frankel, September 9, 2014. Frankel retired at the end of 2016 from his position as Editorial Director in the Department of Publications at the Museum of Modern Art in New York.

11. Vilém Flusser, "On Future Architecture," *Artforum* (April 1989): 13-14.

12. Vilém Flusser, "On An Unspeakable Future," *Artforum* (March 1990): 22-23; Vilém Flusser, "On Future Architecture," *Artforum* (May 1990): 35-36.

13. Vilém Flusser, "On Popes," *Artforum* (March 1990): 25-27.

14. Letter from Vilém Flusser to David Frankel, *Artforum* Correspondence Binder, No. 86, Vilém Flusser Archive.

15. *Artforum* Correspondence Binder, Nos. 84 and 93, Vilém Flusser Archive. See Avital Ronell, *The Telephone Book: Technology-Schizophrenia-Electric Speech* (Lincoln: University of Nebraska, 1989).

Introduction

16. Letter from Vilém Flusser to Charles Miller, September 4, 1987, *Artforum* Correspondence Binder, No. 27, Vilém Flusser Archive.

17. Works by Nancy Dwyer, Rodney Graham, Maura Sheehan, Peter Nagy, Matt Mullican, Tom Radloff, Ana Mendieta, Jessica Diamond, and Glen Baxter were used to illustrate "Curie's Children."

18. Ida Panicelli, Anthony Korner and the editors of *Artforum* (September 1989): 2. The same issue included Barbara Ehrenreich writing about the end of the Moral Majority and Gary Indiana on the cancellation of a Robert Mapplethorpe retrospective at the Corcoran Gallery in Washington, D.C. Panicelli's name first appeared on the masthead as editor of *Artforum* in the March 1988 issue.

19. Ida Panicelli, *Artforum* (September 1991): 2. Ironically, this statement appeared underneath a still for Matthew Barney's video "Delay of Game" (1991), which reinscribed white, heterosexual, male heroism — delivered in the video as a kind of extreme-sports endurance art for the '90s — back into the discourse.

20. Jack Bankowsky, "Slacker," *Artforum* (November 1991).

21. Editor's note published along with Vilém Flusser, "On the Term 'Design,'" *Artforum* (March 1992): 19.

22. Vilém Flusser, "On The Term Design," *Artforum* (March 1992): 19-20.

23. Vilém Flusser, *The Shape of Things: A Philosophy of Design* (London: Reaktion, 1999).

24. Jack Bankowsky, *Artforum* (September 1992): 2.

Martha Schwendener

CURIE'S CHILDREN

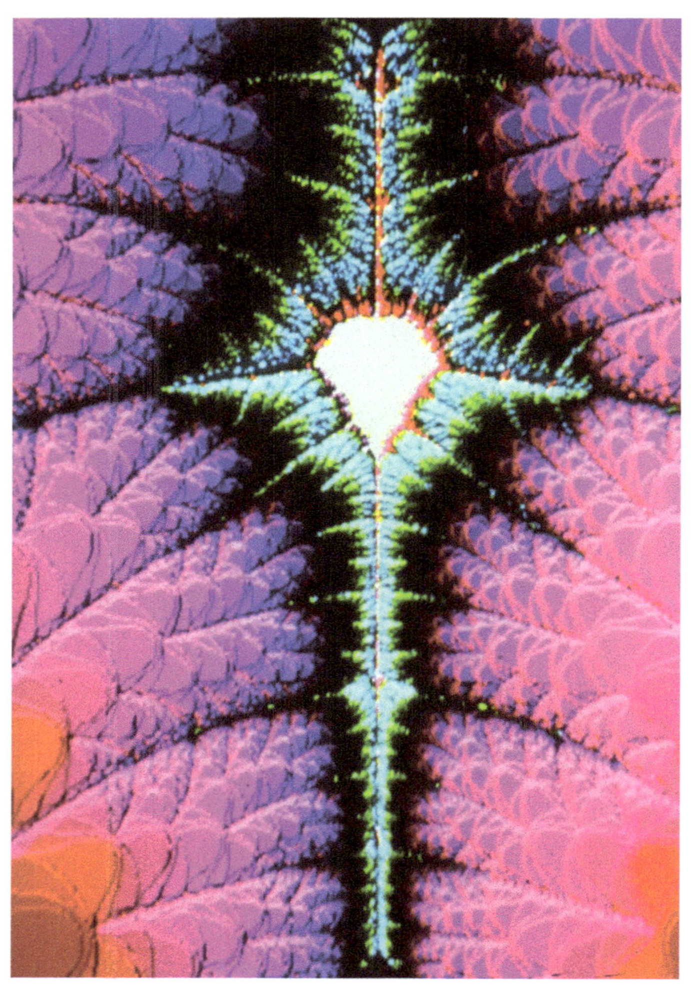

Fractal Pleasure, 1989
Dan Sandin, Electronic Visualisation Lab, University of Illinois at Chicago;
Ellen Sandor & Stephan Meyers, (art)n 11x14" PHSCologram: Cibachrome,
Kodalith and Plexiglas. Courtesy of Ellen Sandor, (art)n.

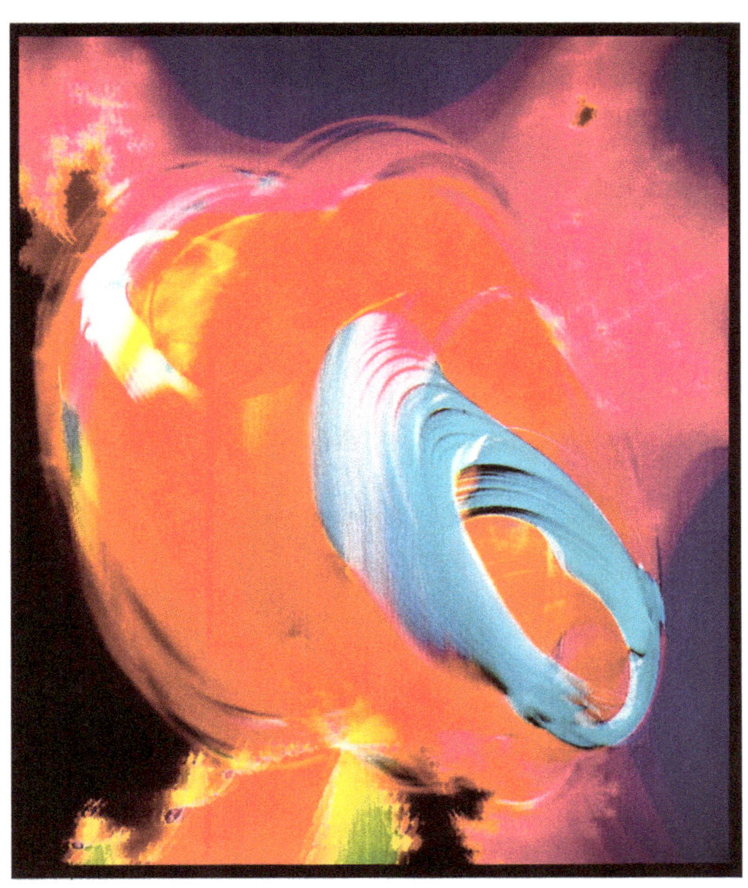

Fourplay, 1990
John Hart, Electronic Visualisation Lab, University of Illinois at Chicago;
Ellen Sandor & Stephan Meyers, (art)n 20x24" PHSCologram: Cibachrome,
Kodalith and Plexiglas. Courtesy of Ellen Sandor, (art)n.

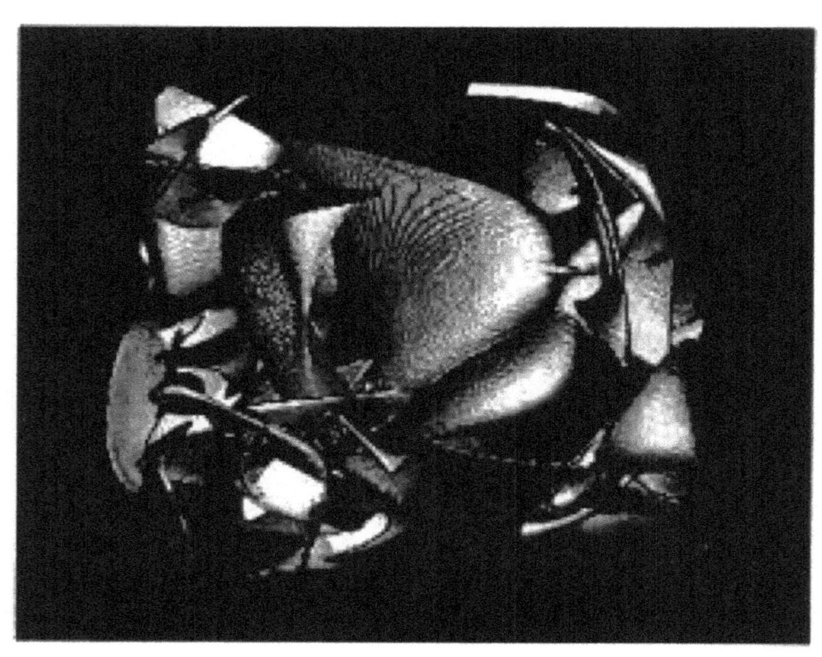

Aspects of Gaia, 1989
Roy Ascott
Computer-generated image by Miles Visman from the "Ars Electronica"
exhibition, Linz, Austria.

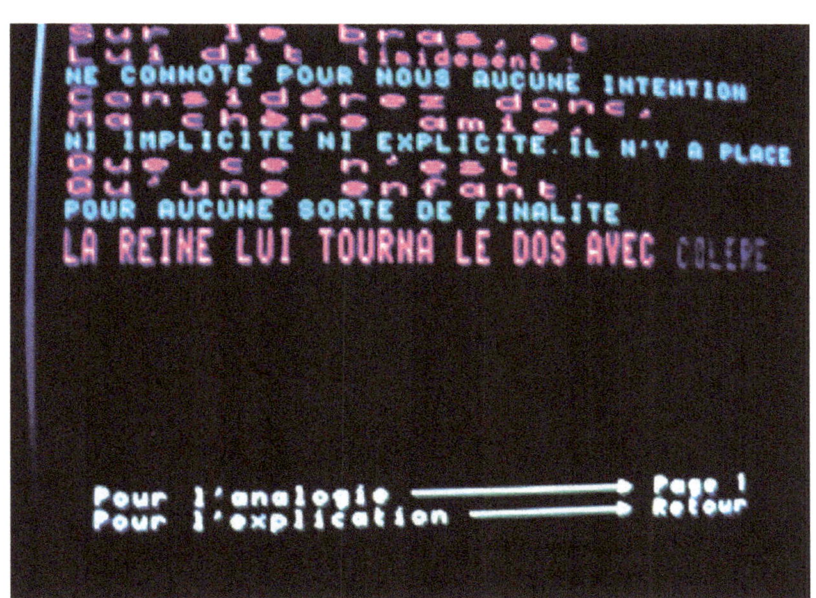

Organe et Fonction d'Alice au Pays des Merveilles, 1985
Roy Ascott
Videotext from the "Les Immateriaux" exhibition,
Centre Pompidou, Paris, 1985.

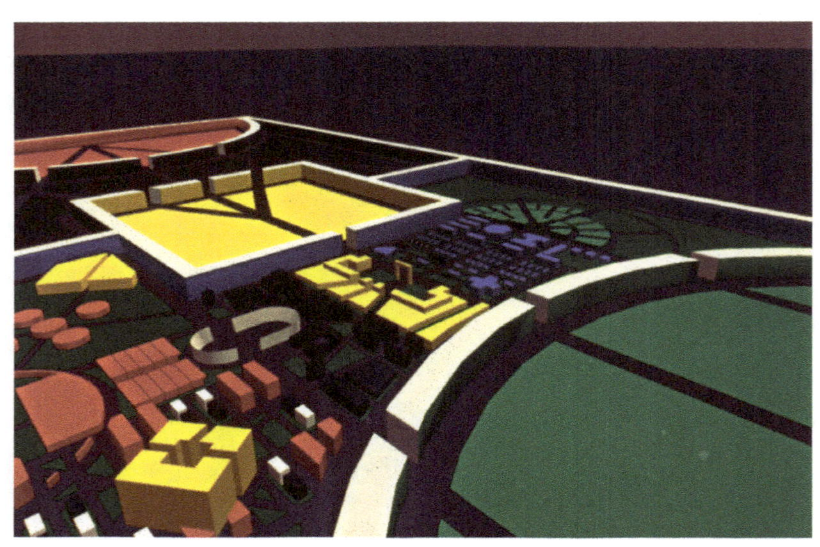

Five Into One, 1991
Matt Mullican
Interactive virtual environment. Courtesy of the artist and
Mai 36 Galerie, Zurich.

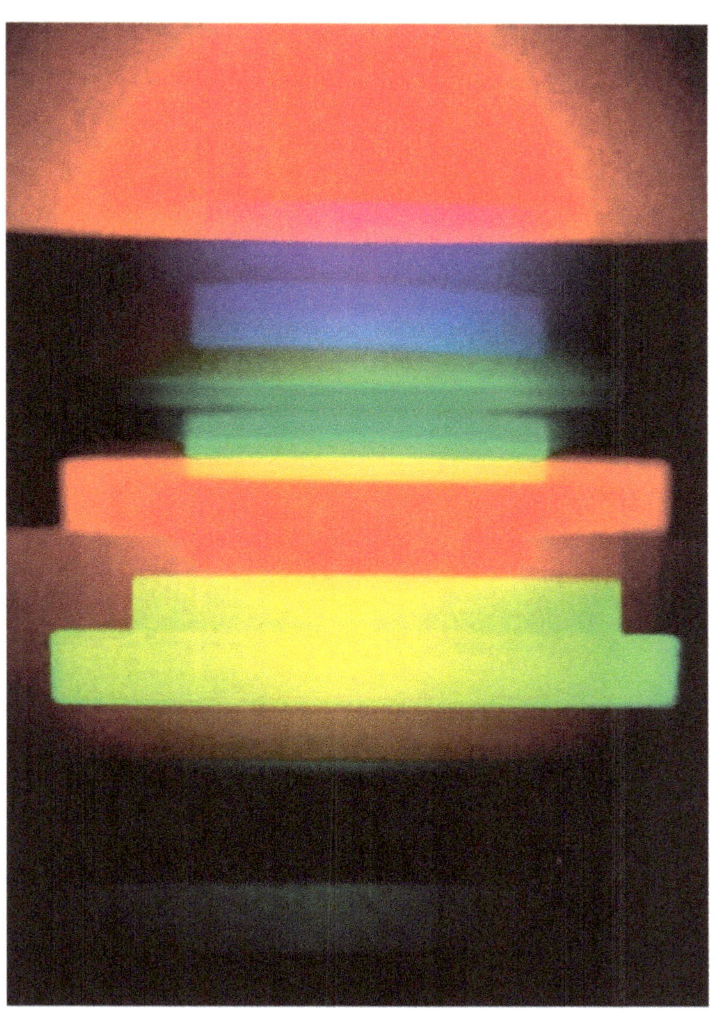

Into the Rainbow, 1983
Dieter Jung
Hologram © ZKM | Center for Art and Media Karlsruhe.

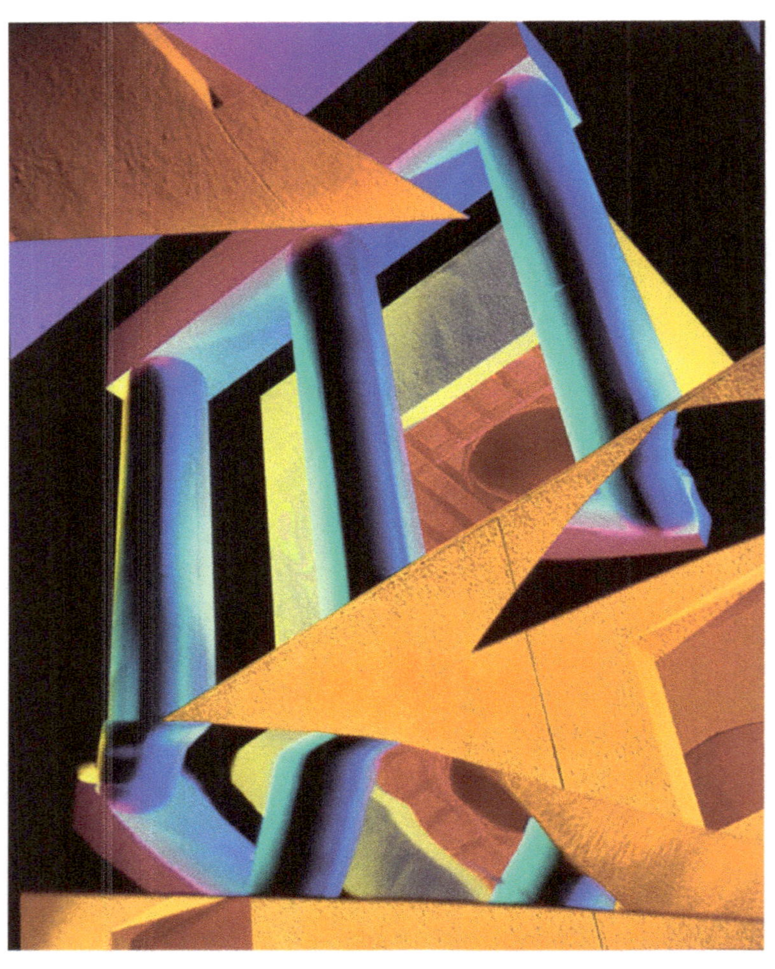

Architectural Site 8, 1986
Barbara Kasten
Cibachrome.

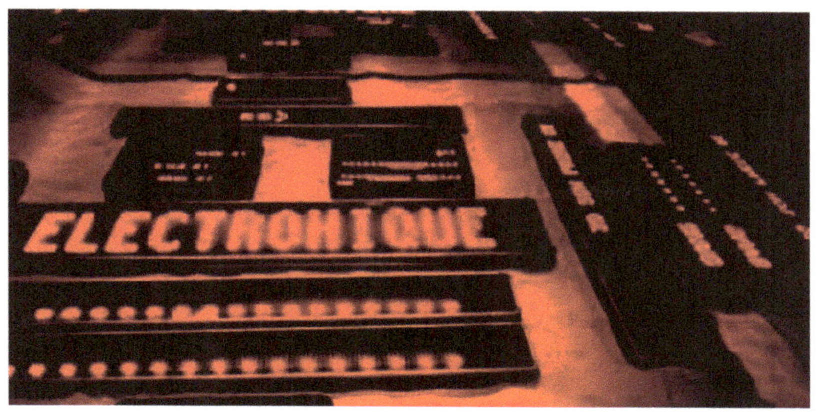

The Electronic Bible and the Persian Gulf War, 1991
Fred Forest
Installation image, National Center for Art and Technology, Reims and La
Base, Levallois-Perret.

ON SCIENCE

Artforum
September
1986

§ We are about to enter the age of electromagnetism. Microelectronics, artificial intelligence, robotics, and holography are some of the signposts on our path away from a material culture and toward an "immaterial" one in which we will concentrate on the processing of rays rather than on the manipulation of inert, perfidious matter. Electromagnetism is about the oscillation of the particles that constitute the rays. Light is such an oscillation. Electromagnetism, then, is about visible and invisible light. What we are about to enter, then, is the true Age of Light. But before we congratulate ourselves on this feat we should consider the implications contained in this metaphor. § We prefer light to darkness, a Manichæism that manifests itself in numerous images: the Buddha as the enlightened One, the halos surrounding the heads of the Christian saints. We can see what sort of light is involved in those images if we look at an Orthodox Eastern icon. It is the light that comes in from the background, the golden light of transcendence. Not everyone approves of this sort of light; certainly the moderns did not, because it makes things appear so dogmatically, and appearances were not to be trusted. The moderns preferred a different sort of light, one that illuminates the scene from the point of view of the viewer, rendering it transparent. Most of the modern metaphors that deal with light — clarification, enlightenment, reflection — mean the awareness projected by the human subject onto the objective world. But we are no longer moderns, and as postmoderns, we do not trust this beam either. We are after a different sort of radiation. § All the modern metaphors for light may be reduced to this: the "light of reason" is a kind of searchlight that will work only if the area at which it is directed is covered by darkness. Once the background light has been switched off, the scene becomes accessible to the searchlight, which first illuminates the foreground (nature), and then penetrates ever deeper into the background darkness (its invisible substructure). It will bring to light, discover and clarify what hides there. It will discover the wires that link and regulate, the laws of nature. But the searchlight of reason sought the true infrastructure of nature for the purpose of achieving power over it. Thus the metaphor "the light of reason" can be seen as a variation of the mythical themes of Lucifer and Prometheus. It is hard to agree with this identification of the light of reason with the devil, because the dream of that light (truth discovered through science) did not suggest hellfire. But at present, when science no longer searches for truth but for falsification, and when technology results in Auschwitz, Hiroshima, and Chernobyl, in thermonuclear devices and in environmental pollution, we are in a position to taste the Luciferian flavour of the light of reason.

§ As for the moderns, some of them did not fully trust the light of reason either, because its torch comes equipped with a curious gadget, a metaphorical mirror that reflects the rays of reason back onto reason itself. This is the business of reflection and speculation, or the critique of reason, which clarifies those dark places where the light of reason originates. And those dark places are indeed infernal ones, as we have found out lately. Two different hells are in fact brought forth by the critique of reason: one that is found by formal, or Wittgensteinian, investigations; the other by existentialism, or Freudianism. The formal hell shows us that all reasonable statements are either true but meaningless (tautologies of the type "it either rains or it does not rain"), or meaningful but false. The existential hell shows us that reason sits upon an infernal brew of repressed desires. Thus it may be said that reason, with its inbuilt mirror, is bound to destroy itself through a sort of feedback: the more its light advances into the darkness beyond, the more it flickers. Still, this did not prevent our modern predecessors from bearing that light forward. § We can do so no longer. Our modern forbearers were a bit too successful in rendering all things transparent, and this triumph of reason was to be its downfall. We can now see through all things, and what we see is a background radiation quite unlike the one switched off when the light of reason began to move forward. The radiation we now see gives off more rays than the transcendent one, as we may find out if we compare an atomic mushroom cloud to the golden background in a Byzantine painting. But this is not what makes electromagnetic radiation so different from transcendent radiation. The difference comes up in two different ways, both of which are uncanny. The background radiation (the electromagnetic field) consists of particles that oscillate, and the light of reason is incapable of clarifying this oscillation; it cannot be switched off, for the light of reason merges with it and has to admit it cannot advance further. What it can do, however, is clarify its own limitation. Thus reason, having discovered radiation, also discovers its own incompetence with regard to it. § But there is more. Neurophysiological research has begun to prove that perception, imagination, sensation, desire, and decision-making can be broken down into chemical and electromagnetic processes in the brain. These processes consist of particles of energy that jump across the intervals, or synapses, between adjacent neurons, which means that the mental processes are in effect a kind of electromagnetic radiation too. This is not merely an empirical, or a theoretical statement. The action of the brain synapse can be simulated in inanimate objects like semiconductors, a simulation that results in artificial intelligence, a form of reason. But no doubt is possible here: this aspect of the light of reason is a background radiation. Such machines calculate, perform logical operations, make decisions, and bring other machines into accord with those decisions, a technological advance which has already begun to have consequences. One is that it is becoming increasingly difficult to distinguish between the products of human and artificial intelligence. Another consequence is that the radical distinction between the mental and the material, between spirit and matter, will become obsolete if it is admitted that both are forms of energy, or radiation. § This is the metaphor that suggests itself to identify this new age: there is an ocean of light, which is partly visible and partly not, and all things are permeated by it. So are we ourselves; our reason is one means by which this ocean of light infuses us. In fact, everything about us, our own bodies, our own minds, are soaked with radiation. The Age of Reason does not know how to understand it all, since the ocean of light is bottomless, and nothing is hidden behind it. Postmodernism is this conundrum of oscillation. It is the play of rays upon rays that we must try and give meaning to if the new Age of Light that we are about to enter is indeed to be a promise of a radiant future. *

ON COMMUNICATION

Artforum
January
1987

§ After centuries of accepting the alphabet as a given, the question of why and how to visualise language is of renewed validity today. It is an obvious response to say that we write in letters precisely so as to avoid writing in ideograms, but why should anyone want to avoid them in the first place? Why take this long detour through language instead of describing ideas directly through images, as the pictographic origins of the alphabet suggest that we once did? Why not write with ideograms instead of letters, as the Chinese do, and as we are beginning to do when we use computer codes, and when we write numbers?

§ The Semitic inventors of the alphabet had an iconoclastic commitment. For thoughts and actions informed by images have a circular structure: as one's eyes circulate over the image surface in order to decipher its messages, so circulate one's thoughts and actions, in a model we might call "magical." The alphabet was to be an instrument to break this magic circle of eternal return and ritual pattern. It was to lead thought and action out and onto a linear track. Thought was to become discursive and abstract, and action to become progressive, as the eye follows the line of a written text. The invention of the alphabet was to open up a new space-time, that of history. § Now how could such a new code be invented? By taking advantage of an ancient code in which thought seems to move in a straight line — the code of spoken language. When we speak, we seem to be somehow outside and above what we are talking about. We seem to be explaining and criticizing ideas. Alphabetic writing renders visual the linear structure of speech, and in the end it resulted in the discourse of the exact sciences and in technology, which permitted literate societies the idea of conquering the world. Discursive thought and progressive action supplanted magical thought and ritual action, and we began to think in terms of history proper. In the current stage of that development, we may wonder whether the invention of the alphabet was indeed such a good thing. The role of spoken language in writing and in the conception of ideas has resulted in a close link between word and idea. So close is the link that we call the rules of thought "logic," which to the Greeks meant both reason and word. Some even doubt whether wordless thoughts are possible (though everyone admits that there are such things as thoughtless words). The link between word and thought has impoverished almost every sort of wordless thought — with the exception of mathematics, which functions through ideograms. (A numeral is a direct image of an idea, even, if a highly abstract one, the figure "2," for example, stands for a pair, the idea of a group of two, while a letter stands for a sound.) Accordingly, we might wonder whether ideograms may lead thought to even more abstract levels than letters (although in a different direction of abstraction), and whether if letters are overcome in the future by some ideogrammatic code, we might expect new levels of abstract thought to develop. § But perhaps, after all, the true reason for the invention of letters was not solely iconoclasm. Perhaps they were invented because spoken language somehow called out for them. Before letters were invented, people thought and spoke in terms of myth. The word "myth" is related to the Latin *mutus,* meaning mute, incapable of correct articulation. (Perhaps speech in those days was a mumble.) Letters render language more articulate, for they press against it and force it to submit to the rules of linear writing. The medium of a writer, before it is language, is the alphabet. The writer expresses him- or herself through letters upon language. Of course, as marble resists the chisel, so language resists the impression of letters. But the battle is essentially an amorous one. The language seduces at the same time that it resists, as the writer finds out what it can do. And it can do astonishing, marvellous things. § Moreover, through writing, the achievements of language can endure. To write is to receive a language as a gift of previous writers, to change that language, and to hand it over to future writers. Through writing then, language flows from writer to writer, and is changed, both in its structure and in its vocabulary, each time it is passed on. Perhaps letters were invented precisely to permit this flow of language from generation to generation, and thus to constitute a precious heritage of our culture, which we are called upon to preserve and to hand on, enriched by our own endeavour. § These are two different answers to the question, "Why letters?" The one says that they were invented to liberate thought and action from pre-historical magical models, the other that they were invented as substitutes for mythical ways of speaking and thinking, thus enabling a clear and progressively refined articulation. These responses are complementary (magic and myth being two faces of the same coin). Both answers affirm that the purpose of letters is to bring about historical consciousness. And, in fact, the invention of alphabetic writing initiated history proper not only because writing records events, but also for the more radical reason that it permits events to be perceived as historical ones, and not as phases of an ever revolving cycle. Western history, then, came about thanks to the writing of letters (if "thanks" is the appropriate word). § Today things are no longer as they were three thousand years ago on the eastern shores of the Mediterranean. We now have instruments that allow us to register speech without using letters, for instance through tapes or records. And we use instruments, for example computers, which permit us to think without the use of letters. These instruments may be programmed by new types of codes that express ideas without having to pass through letters. Perhaps only specialists will have to learn letters in the future, as today only specialists learn Egyptian hieroglyphs or Incan knots. People have been saying for some time that we may be beginning to take leave of literature and to anticipate an illiterate culture. § What will that culture look like? Spoken language will invade the scene day and night from speakers, TV screens, and computer terminals. In this it probably will not be very different from what it was before the invention of letters. This will not matter, however, for language, although omnipresent, will no longer be at the centre of culture, but will form a sort of noisy background. New dimensions of thought will develop, profoundly changing not only ideas but also action. Poetic thought and mathematics will merge in a way that we are as yet unable fully to appreciate, although we can already observe the first results of the merger in synthetic imagery and music. Our children's lives will be as different from ours as ours is different from pre-historical life. And our children's children probably will not feel the absence of literature as a great loss. It is different for us, who fear that the letter, this most precious heritage entrusted to us by our ancestors, will lose its splendour. Those still committed to the writing of letters, despite their belief in the futility of that commitment, may feel that with the loss of this remarkable cultural object life will lose much of its attraction. For them, *scribere necesse est, vivere non est.* Our children's children may think that with the defeat of the cumbersome code of letter, new horizons of thought were opened. Many of us will feel that in taking leave of literature, we are taking leave of many of the noblest values with which we identify ourselves. *

ON DISCOVERY

Artforum
September
1987

§ Every age has its men and women who want to go beyond the conventional wisdom, who want to know better. Through centuries, for example, everyone thought that the substance of things was composed of earth, water, air, and fire, and that ideally these elements would form four perfect spheres, with fire on the outside surrounding air, which in turn would surround water, which would cover the earth. Aristotelian theory essentially said that the behaviour of the elements could be explained as their efforts to stay in the spheres in which they belonged: if a stone is thrown into the air, it falls back to earth; if water sinks into the earth, it returns to the surface as a spring, and if it rises into the air it falls back down as rain; air always lies above both earth and ocean, and flame always rises through air, as if striving upward. Everything seemed clear. Galileo, however, knew better.

§ By arguing that stones fall because the earth attracts them, Galileo challenged ancient philosophical and religious traditions, life experience and logic, as they were understood at the time, and indeed the social system that rested on all these. His challenge was not welcome. Wasn't it more or less the same thing to say that the Earth attracts stones, and to say that they seek their proper place there? How could Galileo have questioned the harmony and beauty of the Aristotelian universe for such a trifling distinction? Today, we understand the huge difference between the two statements, yet Galileo could not have known what the results of his ideas would eventually be. He was simply shocked by the fact that Aristotle and his followers claimed to understand the desire of the elements for their proper place. How could anyone know the motives of a stone? They only believed they did; they took it for granted that there were intentions behind the world. If one looked at things without that belief, one saw not motives but only motions and inertia. Galileo knew better than others, then, because he knew that he knew nothing about motives. He knew better because he knew he knew less. § What does "knowing better" mean, then? Aristotle asked "What do things move for?" and this prevented him from really knowing about motion. By seeing that we cannot know the motives of motion, Galileo was able to ask a better question, "Why do things move?," and got a better answer. Knowing better, then, is distinguishing better between questions. We are still learning about these distinctions. We have learned that it is just as much of a prejudice, after all, to suppose a causality behind the world as to suppose an intention — just as much of a prejudice to ask "Why do things move?" as "What do they move for?" A better path of inquiry might be to restrict ourselves to the question "How do things move?" In doing so, we could for a moment think we have understood why science pursues better knowledge. For while we can never make it rain by asking "What does it rain for?," by asking "How does it rain?" we open up the possibility of making it rain artificially, and thus of alleviating drought and changing the world. Yet to assume that better knowledge is knowledge that changes the world only serves another prejudice — the idea that knowledge has to be functional, that it is worthless in itself. § Let us return to Galileo, who, knowing that he knew less than Aristotle, knew better than Aristotle. But in some ways Galileo actually knew more than Aristotle — he knew that there are mountains on the moon, for example — and his greater knowledge helped him to see how much he did not know. Our great-grandparents believed that the world began in a single act of creation; we know better — we know that we know little of the world's beginnings. As knowledge increases, the relationship between the known and the unknown shifts in favour of the unknown. § This space of the unknown tends to disrupt what was known before, creating gaping holes in the edifice of knowledge, holes that both rupture individual disciplines and separate them from each other. This introduces a new issue, the issue of specialisation: men and women may all be pursuing better knowledge, yet may remain worlds apart from each other in what they know. Let us suppose that in 1492, when Columbus embarked to investigate the blank space that today is filled with the Americas, another mission set sail from China, and somewhere in the middle the two met. Columbus, on his return home, would have announced to the European monarchs that the blank space was more of China; it was, after all, inhabited by Chinese, and he had of course been expecting to reach the Orient. His Chinese counterpart, on the other hand, would have told the emperor that since he had met Europeans on his travels, the blank space had to be more of Europe. Both explorers would have also come up against Aztecs, Incas, and other Native Americans, but to Columbus, believing he was in China, these people would have seemed like curious Chinese, and to the Chinese explorer like curious Europeans. If all this had happened, the Americas would not have been seen as a new discovery; they would have seemed only an extension of what was known before.

§ Consider now, in an analogous way, an expedition that contemporary scientists might send out (or tumble) into the gaping hole we call the origin of Earth's life. Some explorers come in from genetics, others from molecular physics. The European explorers of genetics run into the Chinese explorers of molecules and each believes they are on the other's territory. Each expedition goes home with a few captured Aztecs, respectively labelled molecules and genes, though rather curious ones, in fact, they are neither. Any new knowledge that might have been gained is hidden in a grey zone of assumptions. This is just one example of how specialisation may have rendered it more difficult for us to know when we are learning something new. § We might describe the history of knowledge as follows: first, we knew, then, we knew how much we did not know; then, we began to feel that we did not know what we had thought we knew; and now, perhaps, we can no longer be certain what we know. (And this we call the progress toward better knowledge.) If we can read this history without getting dizzy, it is striking how much it mirrors the history of faith. First, we simply believed; then, we believed, though we knew that belief was not completely logical; then, we began to think that we did not believe; more and more lately we doubt that we do not believe. These two sequences in the vital realms of knowledge and belief are in part why we feel such collective anxiety, both because it really is impossible to know anything without believing in something, and because knowing without believing opens the way for incredible misuse of knowledge. And so our sense of perspective is unhinged. There are those who respond by trying to get away, perhaps through membership of religious sects, or other kinds of denial. The danger is that we retreat from our situation, our disoriented perspective, rather than face it. Perhaps, instead, we should explore the idea that this unfixed perspective is itself a kind of better knowledge, a new space in which to live. *

ON DISCOVERY II

Artforum
October
1987

§ "The spiritual in art," "the spiritual in people" — we inherit and we read and we watch and listen to descriptions of a person, or a thing made by someone, as "spiritual." Such an idea is commonplace, but in reality, of course, we are all mammals, and what we make are the products of mammals. It is true that we have realised certain inventions that sometimes allow us to behave as if we were something different: for a while now we have been able to make machines that we fly like birds, for example, and human females' eggs can now be fertilised outside the womb, like those of fish. As a rule, though, we eat, digest, sleep, copulate, give birth, get sick, and die as apes do. We think we humans are different because of our famous brains. Come to think of it, it is surprising that we have used our brains to change so much about the shape of things in our surroundings but not radically to change the mechanisms that shape the processes of our bodies. Our environment is utterly different from that of the Cro-Magnon, but not our two bodies. That is changing, and what could happen to our bodies is something that relates to art, to the spiritual, and to the artificial. § For some time now we have been trying to improve our mammal condition. During this period we have read all the predictions and warnings that what we have done with automation may eventually transform some of our organs — hands, legs — into appendages fit only for the lightest physical tasks. Genetic engineering promises to transform our grand-children's grandchildren into beings no longer strictly mammal. In the same way, machines will no longer be strictly machines. A combination of neurophysiology and electronics is beginning to project the functions of our brain beyond the skull into computers. Pharmacology may have us experiencing sensations, from vision to orgasm, within our minds, quite independently of our bodies. These are some of the future possibilities; they tend to make the body more subservient to the brain, and thus the irony is that they could indeed eventually make spiritual beings of us. Our immediate instinctual response has been to exaggerate our bodies — by bodybuilding, for example — but with this type of reaction we are just improving our climbing skills. (Climbing is included in our primate program.) § It seems we are moving from the enthusiasm that seized us in the first flush of the new technologies into sober consideration, from being seduced by artificiality into criticism of it, and there is a lot of expression that we do not really like what is happening. Artificial immortality, for example, may be a possibility, and we may like it even less than we like natural death, because we do not know how to live with it. If we were artificially immortal, we would have no reason to live — no reason even to get out of bed in the morning. We are not sure that we want to abandon our mammal condition, not sure that we want to become spiritual beings. No one likes to be mutated; I imagine our ancestors clung with both hands and feet to their branches, and we are just as reactionary about change. It is not that we always love our animal bodies — we sometimes have toothache, for instance. Still, we know the feelings that go with physicality, and we would not want to miss them.

§ When the power of artifice was a figure of speech, we could comfortably see ourselves living in an artificial world. Today, artifice is genuinely powerful, as in artificial kidneys, but we do not necessarily think artificial kidneys are better than natural ones. The moment chemical manure was invented; we claimed the beauty of unfertilised produce. The moment chlorophyll was artificially synthesised we rediscovered natural greenery, and even organised political parties to protect it. Now, when biology has stopped being a natural science and has turned into genetic engineering, we feel more and more concern over endangered species. This is the way of utopias: we want them to stay where they are, namely nowhere. As long as it was utopian to speak about "pure spirit" we could praise spiritual values. Today, pure spirit is on its way. (Is a hologram of a non-existent object a foreshadowing of it?) Now that brains have been on the agenda of the artificial, maybe we can rediscover them too. Would it not be wonderful if the past three or four million years could be seen as a preparatory stage for humanisation, spiritualisation, or whatever name makes us "brilliant"? Then it could be our privilege to be present when humanisation happens — when "true art is born." *

ON DISCOVERY III

Artforum
March
1988

§ Whatever the term "art" may mean at present, it had a different meaning for the ancients. Then, two art forms were held supreme: the art of living, *ars vivendi*, and the art of dying, *ars moriendi*. We have unlearned the second of these, but the first has recently re-emerged in a surprising shape: it is now called "biotechnics." The word seems a Greek-derived version of the Latin *ars vivendi*, but it is quite different in climate from the ancient sense of the term. In fact, it is a discipline out of which a whole world of artificial living beings – living artworks – will arise, and that adventurous world will create a radically different context for our grandchildren's existence.
§ We often consider this development as if it were a new kind of industrial, or computer, revolution: instead of animating inorganic machines, we will animate organisms, and instead of creating artificial intelligences from silicon we will have artificial brains made of nerve fibres. But the biotechnical revolution can also be seen from the viewpoint of art. Whatever

"art" may mean — and setting aside for the moment those artworks that are created to be temporary, or to exist only in the mind — art is always the production and preservation of information. An art object is information stored in some material — stone, bronze, paint — that keeps it from being forgotten. In the end, this is a forlorn purpose. The second law of thermodynamics states that in a closed system, for example the universe that surrounds us, all energy, and thus all information, will in time dissolve and be forgotten. Those who aim at immortality through the production of art, those who believe in the creation of eternal values through art, are on the wrong track.

§ There is, however, a curious material in our universe that seems in a way to defy the universal tendency toward entropy. It is living matter. As far as we know, it exists only on the planet Earth, and there is little hope of finding it elsewhere. This "biomass" forms a sort of slime that covers the globe; its weight can be calculated with some precision. It consists of individual microscopic drops containing information. Those drops tend to divide, and they transmit their information to their successors. During the transmission, variations or mistakes may occur, and the information changes. These mistakes are called "mutations." Thus living matter as a whole carries a stream of ever more diversified information, apparently defying the second law of thermodynamics. It doesn't really, of course – life on Earth is not eternal, and will disappear one day. Still, the duration of Earth's biomass is very considerable. It is to be measured in hundreds of millions of years, not in the millennia that measure art and culture. It is as near to eternal as we can come.

§ Something must be said, however, about the production and transmission of information by living matter: it applies an extraordinarily stupid method. New information – creativity – comes about by mistake, or, if you prefer, by pure chance. Even such marvellous, complex information as the nervous system of an octopus, or the human brain, are the results of blind, haphazard variations. And there is more to the stupidity of biological "evolution." In the course of hundreds of millions of years, the single drops of which the biomass consists have brought about very complicated structures called "organisms"; the human body is one such. But these organisms do not contribute to the diversification of living information. The drops, the germinal cells, flow through organisms as if they were mere channels, and the information the drops contain is not affected by anything the organisms do or suffer. They take no notice of anything in our culture, in our art, and they mutate, they change the information they contain, not by anything we do but only by mistake, by chance, amplified, in Darwin's terms, by natural selection and by the passage of large periods of time. This may be put the following way: there is no possibility of biologically inheriting acquired information. What could be more stupid? § The drops that carry biological information are microscopic, which is why they have been discovered only lately. And the information they carry, molecules of complex acids, are even smaller. Once they were discovered, however, it became possible to manipulate them. This is a shattering statement.

Breaking to bits almost everything we have learned about life, about art, about our position in the world, it says that it has now become possible to create information that can be inserted into living matter, which can become hereditary. It has become possible to create a work of art that will live, will multiply, and will itself create other works of art, practically forever. This is in essence what biotechnics is about — this is the new "art of living." To artists who put information into stone, canvas, paper, celluloid, electromagnetic fields, whatever, must now be added those who can create living beings, and who do so by a method apparently more intelligent than the one that brought us into existence. § At this completely immodest point a word of caution is in order. First, of course, we have no idea where these techniques may lead us or what blunders we may make getting there. Second, the term "creation" may mean two things. One is the production of new information by recombining the elements of the information already available. This one we might call "variational" creation. The other is the production of new information by the introduction of some new element altogether, some "noise." One might say that this is "true" creation. So far, biotechnics has restricted itself to variational creation: it has recombined the elements of available genetic information. If "God" created us, He or She had recourse to the other method, to true creation. But there seems to be no reason why biotechnics should not do the same in the future. § The genetic information that flows through the biomass is all encoded in the same material, nucleic acids, and it all has the same structure, the double helix. Thus all manifestations of life on Earth, be they as different from each other as is a pine tree from a chimpanzee, are variations on the same type of information. Should there be somewhere in space, or even here on Earth, some phenomenon very similar to life processes but encoding information in a slightly different way, we would not recognise it as life. (This is why the search for life in space is a self-defeating endeavour.) So far, to my knowledge, biotechnics is doing the same thing natural evolution does — variational creativity, the sole difference being that it does its work not by chance but according to a deliberate program. Yet there is no reason why the material and the structure of genetic information should not be interfered with in the future. And if even a single atom within a molecule of a nucleic acid were replaced by a different atom, we would have created a form of life as it had never existed before in the world. This would be true creation. § Consider for a moment what this statement implies. It says that we now possess a technique for creating a whole series not just of living beings, though that is remarkable in itself, but of forms of life such as never before existed. Over time, Earth's biomass has produced complex nervous systems, and thus sensations, perceptions, desires, thoughts, decisions — all our and other species' mental processes. We now possess a technique that permits us to create the foundations of mental processes that have never before existed, processes for which words like "sensation," "perception," "desire," "thought," and "decision" are inappropriate, since they describe only processes we already know. In short, the statement that we can now create new forms of life implies that we can now create "spirits" that we are incapable of understanding. § Is this not a description of magic, and of the magical power that is said to characterise artistic creation? Is it not said of art, by romantics and not-so-romantics, that it creates what has never existed before ("originals"), that it brings things to life, that it results in something its very creator is incapable of understanding? So far, all such affirmations have been metaphors. With, biotechnics, they become literally true. This new "art of living" enables us to become not just metaphorically but literally creative. Thus it might be said that biotechnics is art in the literal sense of the term. § If we consider the future as it begins to emerge from the mists of the two revolutions we are witness to — the "telematic," or computer and media, revolution and the biotechnical revolution — we are impressed by the fact that they promise a world where life may be calculated, programed, and computed. But what is even more impressive is the promise that we may become truly creative artists, masters in the art of living. With this curious reservation, however: we shall be incapable of understanding the spirits to which we shall be giving life. *

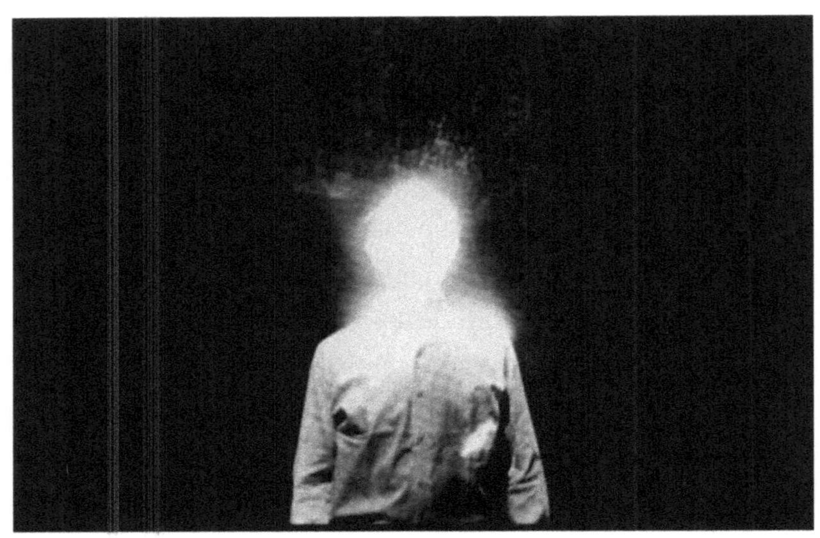

The Illuminated Man, 1969
Duane Michals
Gelatin silver print.

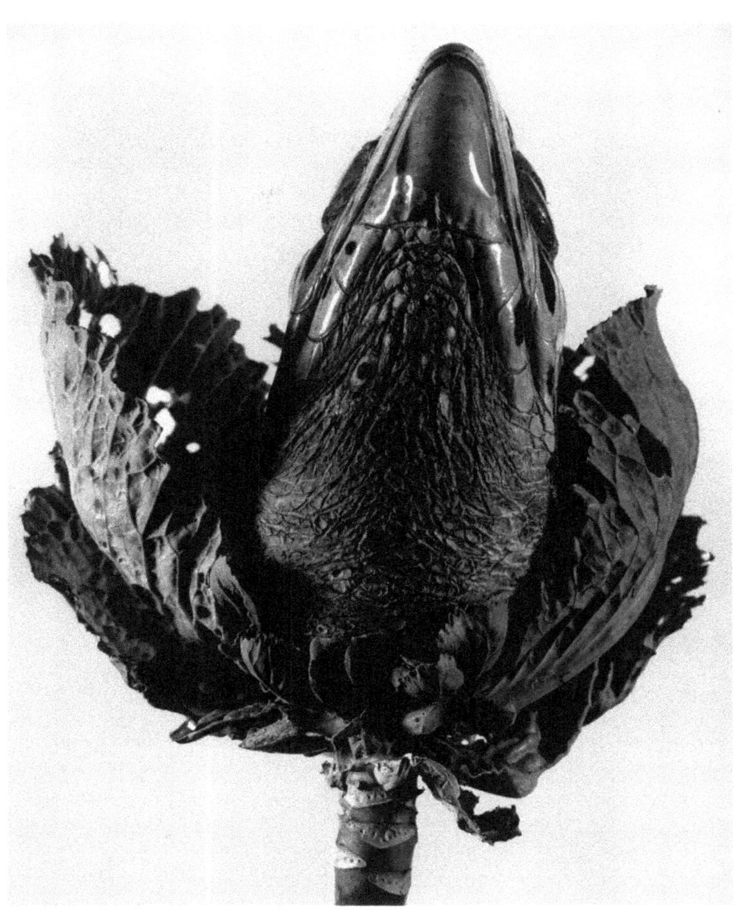

Lavandula Angustifolia, 1984
Joan Fontcuberta
Gelatin silver print.
From Fontcuberta's *Herbarium* series of imaginary plants.

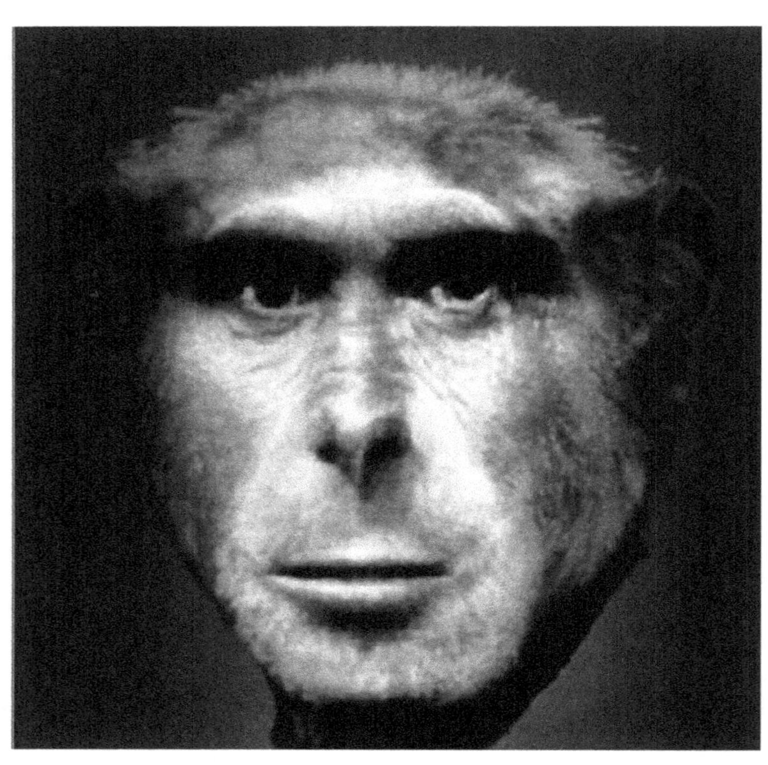

Evolution II: Chimpanzee and Man, 1984
Nancy Burson
Gelatin silver print from computer-generated negatives.

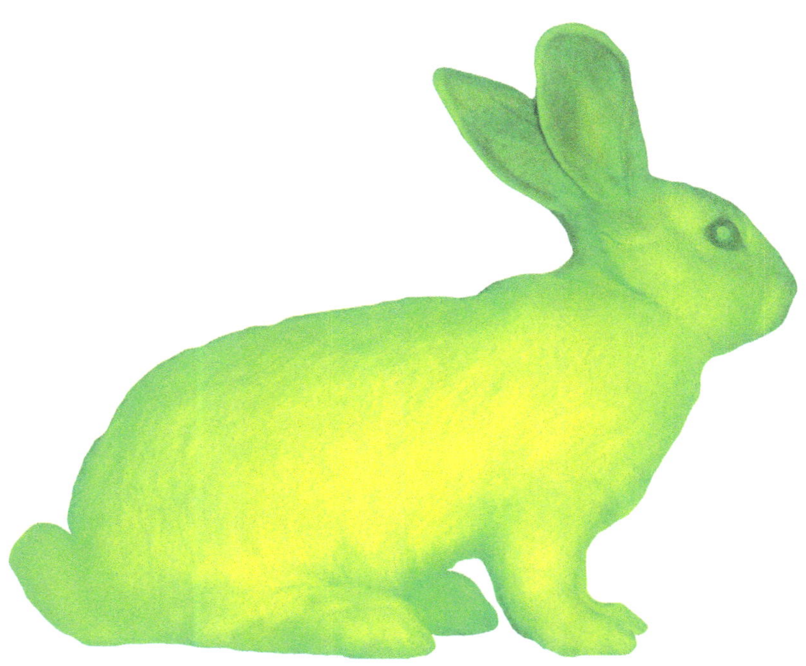

GFP Bunny, 2000

Eduardo Kac

Transgenic rabbit created with EGFP, a synthetic mutation of the green
fluorescent gene found in the jellyfish Aequorea Victoria that glows under
correct lighting. Made with the assistance of Louis Bec.

ON DISCOVERY IV

Artforum
April
1988

§ *Homo sapiens'* curious ability to make pictures of the world may be observed in images on cave walls that coincide with the earliest days of human consciousness. Lately, however, a new capacity is emerging — we can now make pictures of calculations, and these may be observed in images on computer screens. Both these capacities manifest themselves in the shape of pictures, but they should be distinguished from each other. If they are not, we risk missing the point of the cultural revolution of our time. § To make a picture of something in the world, one must step back from it. The question is, Where to? It is easy to answer, from one place to another. If one wants to make a picture of a pony, for instance, as the cave artists did in the Dordogne, one must watch it from a certain distance and vantage. But we know from experience that this is not the whole answer. When making a picture, we not only observe but also imagine. We step back from the world into ourselves, into somewhere not so much a place as a nonplace. Our imagination is our capacity to withdraw from the world to that nonplace. (This is not an explanation, just a description, because although we use our imaginations every day, it is almost impossible to say how.) When making a picture, then, we are no longer within the world (we no longer *in-sist*), we are outside it (we *ex-sist*). We have become subjects in an objective world. § This is an uncomfortable situation. As subjects, we do not have arms long enough to bridge the abyss between the world and ourselves. Imagining things in the world, we cannot seize them and handle them. The world is no longer manifest; it has become apparent. It is no longer composed of objects against which we stumble; it is composed of phenomena that we look at. Why did we put ourselves in this uncomfortable position, the position of doubt, of alienation? We did it in order to see the world as a context. We wanted to see the forest as well as the trees. Having seen the world as a context from or through our imaginations, we may seize and handle it better when stepping back into it than we did before. Imagination is a process of *réculer pour mieux sauter*, and pictures are, among other things, orienting tools for seizing and handling the world better. § An additional remark seems in order. To imagine, to step back from the world into "existence," is not sufficient for making pictures. What one has seen one must somehow fix, for instance on cave walls or canvases, and one must somehow codify it in a form in which it will become meaningful for others. In other words, one must feed one's imagination into a memory (to use a computer term), and one must render it intersubjective. This is the process of producing pictures. My interest here, however, is not in art's vocabulary of forms and techniques, nor in, say, the question of abstract art, which is a whole question in itself, and which might be considered an intermediate stage between the old and the new ways of thinking. My interest is in these two different forms of imagination. § The new imagination involves the capacity to make pictures of calculations. Most of us have no experience of it, and in the absence of concrete experience, elegant concepts like "existence" and "subjectivity," which are so useful in discussion of the old imagination, become meaningless terms. Instead, we must describe what the possessors of the new imagination actually do. Facing an apparatus equipped with a keyboard and a screen, they press the keys, and pictures appear on the screen. Where do they sit, and why do they do what they do? These are the questions we ask of the old imagination. There, the answers are that people sit in "subjectivity," in "existence," and they do what they do (make pictures) in order to seize and handle the world better. People with common sense (reactionaries) will answer the same way about the new imagination, because for them there is nothing really new under the sun. But the question is not so simple.

§ The old imagination produces pictures of things. In part because of their very subjectivity, however, these pictures are not clear, distinct models, and may not offer any obvious instruction as to how to proceed. To clarify them, we use writing, which was invented, some three thousand years ago, in order to explain (tell) pictures, to "de-cipher" them, and thus to permit an orderly handling of the world. But writing is linear, it follows the order of the line, and the line is not always the best way to pass through the world. Linear orders — classical logic, or causal explanations — do not always properly describe events. This is why, with the invention of calculus some three hundred years ago, the lines of writing were cut into points and intervals. The purpose of calculus is to permit a minutely exact seizure and handling of the world. One of the results of calculus is those devices whose keys are pressed by those with the new imagination. § What we seem to have here is a sort of loop: first, images produced by the old imagination were analyzed into lines by writing, then those lines were analysed into points by calculus, and now those points are being resynthesised into images by the new imagination. That loop has taken three thousand years to unfold, and one is tempted to say that it closes a circuit in Western civilisation. But do those who possess the new imagination now sit somewhere outside Western civilisation, or do they do what they do as a way of restoring the prehistoric magic of Lascaux? Clearly not. The matter must be examined further. § The first picture to be synthesised from points is the photograph, in its modern form a sediment of silver grains suspended in gelatine. It is true that every earlier picture, and every object in the world, can also be said to be grainy – composed of molecules, atoms, and even smaller point-like bits. But photos are the first pictures made through the deliberate, non-manual assembly of such bits. They are the first manifestations of the new imagination, and they are the place of departure for our examination. § The silver grains of which a photo consists are too small to be assembled by hand. Equipment must be designed to do it, designed in such a way as to capture light in the silver molecules and then compute it into pictures. This equipment can function automatically, without human intervention. (A photographer may press the shutter release, of course, but he or she is an unnecessary substitute for an automatic shutter.) What is the purpose of all this? The question should not have been asked of the early camera inventors, and even less of the photographers: they did not know what they were doing. Only now, when we possess synthetic computer images, can we answer the question. Typically of the workings of technology, the computer should not be seen as a consequence of the camera, as if the camera were its cause; rather, the camera should be taken as a primitive computer.

§ It now appears that cameras were invented in order to emancipate the human imagination from the need to make pictures, and to free it for the programming of computers to produce pictures automatically. The new imagination programs a computer and then waits while the computer vomits images. Some of these images will surprise the programmer: they are unexpected. They are "informative" pictures, improbable pictures. Withdrawing from actual picture-making, into picture-making through programming, the human imagination has become more powerful, more informative. It can amplify itself through the computer, using the computer to create images it could not generate itself.

§ But this is not the whole truth about the new imagination. As imagination withdraws from picture-making into programming, it somehow reverses itself. For the pictures that it creates point in the opposite direction from those produced by the old imagination. The old imagination withdraws from the world into a nonplace from which it produces pictures. It thus describes a motion of abstraction: from the world, from the three-dimensional, it abstracts the two dimensions of the picture surface. The new imagination advances from the points of the calculus toward the production of pictures. It is thus a motion of concretion: it projects from the abstract, the zerodimensional, into the two dimensions of the picture surface. The old pictures are orienting tools within the world: they point at the world, they show it, they mean it. The new ones are projections of calculating thought: they point at thought, they show it, they mean it. § Now thought itself does not mean the world as it is, but the world as it could be. A synthetic computer-produced picture of an airplane shows not a "real" airplane but a possible one. It is the representation of a "thought" plane. Thus we no longer face the world as its underlings, as "sub-jects." We now possess the ability to calculate the world as a field of virtualities, and to compute some of those virtualities into simulations of realities according to our own program. This is the new imagination. The consequence is that we no longer manipulate the things of the world in order to change the real, but that we do so in order to realise virtualities. We are no longer "sub-jects," but "pro-jects." One's head spins in trying to grasp this existential revolution. § My argument here may seem a rather elaborate formulation. It is not. Those who are committed to the production of the new pictures experience it concretely. A curious creative dizziness takes hold of those who program synthetic pictures, who possess the new imagination. With each key they press, they dive into a field of virtualities. Entire worlds emerge that they themselves had not expected. A new level of existence is opening up, with new experiences, sentiments, emotions, concepts, and values proper to it. *Homo sapiens* is about to bring a faculty into play that so far has only been dormant. ✻

ON DISCOVERY V

Artforum
June
1988

§ The Greek word "morphogenesis," which means "birth of form," would have had a curious sound to classical ears. The understanding of the time would have questioned how forms could be born — were they not timeless? By looking at the world, the ancient Greek could see that this was so. Take cows, for example: each cow is born and dies, but the form of the cow is always the same, and it somehow passes from animal to animal with only marginal distortion. The form "cow" is a timeless container through which each individual cow flows; anyone interested in cows should consider the form, and not the shapeless content that moves through it.

§ This concentration on forms the ancient Greeks called "theory," and it was the foundation of their philosophy and science. According to theory, the timeless forms were stored somewhere, ordered according to a logical system. Try reimagining heaven as a set of cupboards. The "higher" forms are stored in the higher cupboards, the "lower" ones below. Logically, one can recover each form from the shelves, one after the other, as they stand arranged in heaven. A potter, say, who wants to mold clay into a shape, must deduce how to reveal something already present in the heavenly cupboard. § We do not do things this way today — instead of discovering shapes, we "invent" or "create" them. Our artists are "creative" (or at least they hope they are). Part of the reason may be that we no longer think of forms as timeless. Since the classical period, the world has grown older by far more than the 2000 or so years that have passed in the interim; we have learned to measure its age in tens of billions of years. In this context, man, that inhabitant of the island of meters, seconds, and other dimensions comprehensible in human terms, can no longer serve as the measure of all things. And from this perspective, forms show themselves to change with time — they become unstable. Over millions of years the body of the cow changes with evolution; the current shape of the universe is a transitory stage between its shape just after the Big Bang and the state into which it is heading. According to the second principle of thermodynamics that state will be without form, since the universe tends progressively to lose all its forms to entropy. § Now if forms can change with time, theory may be understood not as a contemplation of form but as a shaping of it. This is where morphogenesis becomes an issue. In art, in fact, it develops into an absolutely basic problem. Art becomes, among other things, a way of "creatively" producing hitherto nonexistent forms. Instead of imitating forms (mimesis), it invents them (poeisis). The artist becomes godlike. That does not last long, however, since morphogenesis poses the question of how a new form is born. Is it possible to create something absolutely unprecedented? Given that we cannot get to where we are going from any place other than where we are now, that seems unlikely – the greatest leap (and great leaps are certainly achievable) will contain some trace of its jumping-off point. As I have written in these pages before, we have two principal ways of creating new form. First, several old forms can be combined into a new one. The method is old: the ancient Greek Chimera, for example, combined the forms of a goat, a lion, and a serpent. (Presumably there was a Chimera somewhere in the heavenly cupboard.) And today we have the geep, a genetically engineered derivation of the goat and the sheep. Alternatively, something new can be added to an old form — to a chess game, for example, one might introduce a new piece (an elephant, say) between the knight and the castle, completely changing the game. The first model we might call "variational creation," and it is the method of a lot of the work now being done with computers. The second — "true creation," or perhaps "transcendental creation" — seems more the province of the "genius"; we might suppose that an artist — or a genetic engineer, or any kind of "creator" for that matter — is the more godlike the more he or she has access to it. § If we study the matter closely, however, we find we are in trouble. First, consider biological morphogenesis as an example of variational creation. Every shape in which Earth's living beings could manifest themselves is encoded within the existing genetic information as a potential, a virtuality. Some of these shapes become apparent, become real, with the passage

of time, which produces variations in the shapes of these living creatures and thus realises some of their different possibilities of form, whether by chance or, as in the case of the geep, through other complex factors. Since the sum of the Earth's genetic information is limited, the sum of these virtual shapes is limited, but it is a very large sum. It is probably larger than the sum of the molecules that constitute the universe.
§ The duration of the universe is also limited — eventually it will lose all form, both its own and those it contains. (The forms of life on Earth will disappear much earlier than those of the stars and planets.) Thus many of the possible shapes of the Earth's living things will certainly never become apparent, will never be realised, even if we were to accelerate evolution through computer assisted genetic engineering. Thus it appears that variational creation may never exhaust its virtualities. It constitutes, then, a very challenging commitment.
§ Now consider transcendental creation. We have said it involves the combination of a new element with an old form. But where does that new element come from?

It must be preexisting, for it is impossible to add to the universe's sum of matter and energy. To be "new," then, it must simply be new to the form with which it is to be joined. The two kingdoms of animals and plants, for example, never cross over into each other. Something like an exchange may occasionally happen — certain algae, for example, seem to serve as sensory organs for certain oysters — but this is more an example of cooperation than of true intermingling. Now if you could put sight into wheat, or leaves into horses, would that not be transcendental creation? You would have added something new — a "noise," to use the language of modern communication — to an old form, to produce a new one.

§ Since wheat equipped with eyes, or horses with leaves, may be expected never to arise from natural evolution, the person who created them would be a godlike artist, a genius. But let us not get too excited about this. If you produced horses with leaves (horses capable of photosynthesis), you would have made something much less interesting than, say, horses equipped with wings (horses capable of flying). In the first case you would have broken the rules of evolution; in the second you would have stretched those rules to the limit. But if variational creation is in effect inexhaustible, why do we need to resort to transcendental creation? By what right do we break the rules of the game, and at what risk? And even if the consequences were negligible, games are more fun when we stick to the rules; to win by breaking them is not to win at all. § Art, of course, is not only biology, and we tend to accept and even to expect its breaking of the rules. As the creator of form, the artist is committed against the universe's tendency toward the indistinctness of entropy. Of course nature does produce variety of form – the Earth's life is proof – but with the millennia these forms will lose their individuality, and in any case they are produced by chance. We have tended to want our artists to be geniuses, expressing their spirit through the "transcendental creation" of new forms. Those men and women who work with computers to vary preexisting forms, for all kinds of reasons besides aesthetic ones, have seemed less "original" to us. But they are no less concerned with the proliferation of forms than is the genius. And their creation of form is methodical and deliberate, even in its play with chance. For all the interesting work being done with computers today, there remains a residual reluctance to accept them as a medium of expression; eventually, however, we may come to see them as infused with spirit. ⁎

ON SCIENCE II

Artforum
October
1988

§ Why is it that dogs are not yet blue with red spots, and that horses do not yet radiate phosphorescent colours over the nocturnal meadows of the land? Why hasn't the breeding of animals, still principally an economic concern, moved into the field of aesthetics? It is as if nothing in the relationship between humanity and the biological environment had changed since the life-style revolutions of the Neolithic age. Yet at the same time that the farms of North America and Western Europe are today producing more food than we can consume, we also, not coincidentally, have learned techniques that ultimately make conceivable the creation of plant and animal species according to our own program. Not only do we have mountains of butter and ham, rivers of milk and wine, but also we can now make artificial living beings, living artworks. If we chose, these developments could be brought together, and farming could be transferred from peasants, a class almost defunct anyway, to artists, who breed like rabbits, and do not get enough to eat. § If you could make a film of the European landscape that covered the millennia of history but compressed them into a convenient half hour for the comfort of the public, it would show the following story: first, a cold steppe, populated by large ruminant animals migrating northward in spring and southward in the fall, and followed by the beasts of prey, including humans, that hunted them. Then, an ever-denser forest, inhabited by no-longer-nomadic peoples living and working in clearings kept open by the use of stone tools and fire. Then, a basically familiar scene of fields of edible grains, and pastures of edible animals, with occasional forests surviving as sources of newsprint. And if you could project your movie camera into the immediate future, you would see a continent-sized Disneyland full of people working very short weeks because of automation, and trying desperately to amuse themselves so as not to die of boredom. The question is: Who will be the Disney of the future? He or she might, I suggest, be a molecular biologist. § All the organisms of the Earth are coloured. We all secrete dyes in our skins, and these dyes have important functions: they support not only the individual (protective coloration) but the species (sexual signals). We are now beginning to understand the chemical and physiological processes of these secretions, and to be able to formulate the laws that govern them. Molecular biologists may soon be handling skin colour more or less as painters handle oils and acrylics. Then the internal dyes of animal and vegetable biology may acquire a crucial new use: they may help the human species to survive its boredom by filling the future-as-Disneyland with multicoloured fauna and flora.

§ Please do not think this a fanciful conceit. Instead, take scuba gear and a torch, and jump into a tropical ocean. Down deep you will see fields and forests of plant-like creatures whose red, blue, and yellow tentacles sway with the currents, gigantic rainbow-colored snails trailing through the scenery, and swarms of silvery, gold, and violet fish overflying it. This is what our familiar *terra firma* may someday look like. It has almost become feasible to transfer the genetic information that programs deep-sea colouring into the inhabitants of the Earth's surface. You might say that this painting of the future is a kind of land art, but of a much more complex type than the one we know. Instead of wrapping rocks in fabric or showing them around with bulldozers, we may be able to compute and compose a complex living game. There is a kind of potato that is pollinated by a single species of butterfly, which itself feeds exclusively on that potato. The butterfly may be said to be the potato's sexual apparatus, and the potato the butterfly's digestive system, the two forming a single organism. In this particular symbiosis, the butterfly's wing is exactly the same blue as the potato flower. The wing colour results from the reflection of sunlight by minuscule mirrors, that of the flower from the transformation of chlorophyll, but nevertheless they match, the consequence of a complex evolutionary chain of feedbacks and adjustments. The Disney of the future should be able to program such effects at will. He or she may perhaps compose an enormous colour symphony, evolving spontaneously through endless variations (mutations), in which the colour of every living organism will complement the colours of every other organism, and be mirrored by them. A gigantic living work of art, of a wealth and beauty as yet unimaginable, is definitely possible. Today's environmentalists and ecologists, who stubbornly continue to call themselves "green," will object that a landscape transformed into a Disneyland, a work of art, will no longer be "natural." But consider: when these early peoples opened clearings in the forests, they began to make the landscape "artificial." When they planted fields, they accelerated the artifice. The future Disneyland will simply continue it. And anyway, why cannot art inform nature? When we ask why dogs cannot be blue with red spots, we are really asking about art's role in the immediate future, which is menaced not only by explosions both nuclear and demographic, but also equally by the explosion of boredom. *

ON SCIENCE III

Artforum
December
1988

§ We have, of course, quite a number of colour theories, and of techniques that apply them. Surprisingly, however, we seem to have no satisfactory theory on the cultural role of colours. No doubt the symbolic standing of various colours in different cultures has been the subject of ethnological, anthropological, and psychological studies, and the results have surely been applied by people in such fields as publicity, marketing, architecture, and design. But we seem to have no meaningful theoretical answers to questions like, is there, or is there not, an underlying pattern to the periodic changes in colouring of our cultural landscape? Why does the classical Greek town seem to have been so colourful, and the Hellenistic one so monochromatic? What is the explanation for the greyness we associate with 19th century cities (coal? money? printed matter?), and can Impressionism be understood as a revolt against it? Why are capitalistic societies so much more colourful than "people's democracies," even in "colourful" places like

China and Cuba? § Any cultural theory of colours would have to consider them as the elements of information-bearing codes. In traffic, for instance, red means, "stop" and green means, "go," in a code that is valid worldwide. Now codes — the assignment of ordered meanings to particular phenomena — have so far been used essentially to carry information from person to person. We have agreed on certain drawings, for instance, to constitute the code of writing. Today, however, codes are needed to carry information from people to machines — computers, or robots. The digital code is an example. § Machine codes must be clear and distinct, because machines are not made to decipher hidden or ambiguous meanings, as humans do when they read poetry or look at painting. And the issue of the clarity of the codes that mediate between humans and machines beats back upon the codes that mediate between humans. Is it possible, or desirable, to establish interpersonal codes — colour codes, for example — that would be both as articulate as the codes we have devised to talk to machines, and also as unambiguous? Could a colour code become a sort of universal Esperanto, complementing or even substituting for spoken and written language?

§ Generally, codes are built in one of two ways: they are "denotative" or "connotative." In a "denotative" code each symbol "means" a single element among the meanings that the code exists to convey, and each element of that universe of meaning is represented by a single symbol. Such a code is said to be "bi-univocally" related to its universe of meaning. In a "connotative" code, each symbol may "mean" several elements of the universe of meaning, and each element of that universe may be represented by several symbols. Such a code is said to be "equivocally" related to its universe of meaning. Except in a few relatively recent instances, such as the traffic light, or color-coded price tags, colors have so far mainly been used equivocally — for example in painting. § Denotative codes have the merit of clear meanings, and are often used in scientific communication. The system of numbers is a denotative code. But they have the disadvantage that their ability to convey meaning is "poor": they are somewhat inflexible, being unable to evoke the content of whatever intervals fall between their symbols (for instance between "1" and "2"). Through these intervals, large parts of the universe of meaning escape. In connotative codes, on the other hand, meaning is "rich," as the vectors of meaning cross and overlap. This is why they are used in artistic communication; the colours of painting are a connotative code. But connotative systems have the disadvantage — or perhaps the merit — that their meanings are ambiguous, and demand interpretation. § Could a code be made that was both clear and "rich," and if so, could colours be used in it? Could we establish a colour code, or perhaps several, that would serve for both scientific and artistic communication, thus doing away with the fateful divorce between scientific and "humanistic" culture? So stated, the problem shows its revolutionary impact. If such a colour code were feasible, it would radically transform our cultural situation, affecting our thinking, our feeling, our whole perception of the world. It would alter our *aistheton* — would be an aesthetic revolution. § Let us look at the "poverty" of denotative codes. Descartes asked: How can the clear and distinct structure of mathematical thought become adequate to the concrete compactness of the objective world? How can the "thinking thing" (*res cogitans*) become adequated to the "extended thing" (*res extensa*)? His answer was: Through analytical geometry, which to him was the only means for the gaining of scientific knowledge. The method was improved by Leibniz's and Newton's invention of calculus, which was intended to stop up the intervals between the numbers by "integrating the differentials" – by producing a code that could express variability and change. This code, then, was both clear and "rich," and people believed that it would make the world newly accessible to knowledge. One of the reasons our optimistic grandparents believed in "progress" was that everything had become codifiable in differential equations. (This, I would argue, was the true basis of 19th century optimism.) But the optimism did not last, because to apply such equations, to use them to solve problems, it was necessary to renumerise them – to translate from the symbols of higher mathematics into what are usually called natural numbers, a tedious and lengthy task. (It may take longer than the human life span.) This is why computers were invented: to "calculate" equations. And this is the true reason for our contemporary pessimism about "progress": even working up to computer speed, we cannot hope to live long enough to solve all the problems. § We should also consider the curious fact that thinking in the occidental tradition is mostly verbal. The problem that Descartes was trying to solve was one of adequating fundamentally verbal thought ("concepts") to the world. This was because he saw the "thinking thing" essentially as a "speaking thing," a thing that articulated itself through the alphanumerical code. It never occurred to him that one could think nonverbally — for instance in colours. § Of course, it is easy to explain why so much of our thinking is verbal. Since our body's organs allow us easily to codify airwaves into phonemes, speaking comes "naturally" to us (though it is an open question whether speech is a "natural" human faculty or a "cultural" one). Other species, however, have organs that allow them to codify colours. Some cephalopods, for instance, may change the colour of their skin, producing various spots of different hues. They control each spot through their central nervous system, and there is no question but that they use this faculty to communicate; they dispose of a colour language. § But we can do the same, and indeed we have done, at least since Lascaux, or since we began painting on cave walls. We are perfectly capable of thinking in colours, and of thinking nonverbally (illogically). But our colour codes have so far been mostly connotative, and therefore of little value for communicating scientific knowledge. If we were to establish more denotative colour codes, would that affect Descartes' problem of adequating the thinking thing to the extended thing? What sort of knowledge would a color thinking convey, and generate? Would it justify a renewal of optimism? § Today, a fractal equation can be fed into a computer, where it is digitally transcoded, then "numerised" and computed in the form of curves and surfaces on the screen. Those shapes may be adequated to colours: the computer commands a palette of almost infinite variation. What has happened here is that numbers have been chromatically transcoded. A colored image of a fractal equation – let us call it a "Mandelbrot monster," after one of the originators of the science of fractals – is both a model of scientific knowledge (it is as clear and distinct as the code of numbers) and a model for aesthetic experience (it is rich in meaning, like a work of art, which indeed it is). In proposing this kind of colour code, we have lifted both scientific knowledge to the level of aesthetic experience and artistic experience to the level of scientific knowledge. And we have eliminated the distinction between art and science. What we are doing here is thinking scientifically in colours. § Open any issue of Scientific American and you will see other examples of the codification of colour to convey exact knowledge. Computer simulations of nuclear, chemical, and physiological phenomena come to mind, and also the tinting of photographs taken from satellites to show crops, the weather, and so forth. What is lacking in all these efforts, however, is a satisfactory cultural theory of colours. As long as we lack such a theory, the idea of a colour code both clear and "rich" enough that in the future people will be able to communicate through it (as well as or even instead of through words) remains utopian. This is one of the reasons for a project under consideration to build a "House of Colour," a *Casa da Cor,* in Brazil, in the city of São Paulo — a place where a cultural theory of colours might be elaborated. There is as yet no consensus among the scientists, artists, philosophers, and scholars of communications who collaborate in the project as to how such a theory is to be formulated. This, of course, increases their feeling of adventure. § The divorce between the sciences and the arts grows partly from the contempt in which science holds everything not exact, partly from the artist's contempt for the supposed barrenness and poverty of scientific reasoning. If colours could be used as codes for exact communication, those prejudices would disappear. The heart has reasons that reason ignores, and reason has a heart that the heart ignores, and only a unification of the two can really develop the virtualities dormant within all of us. Colour may be a place where those two can meet, and result in a new culture. *

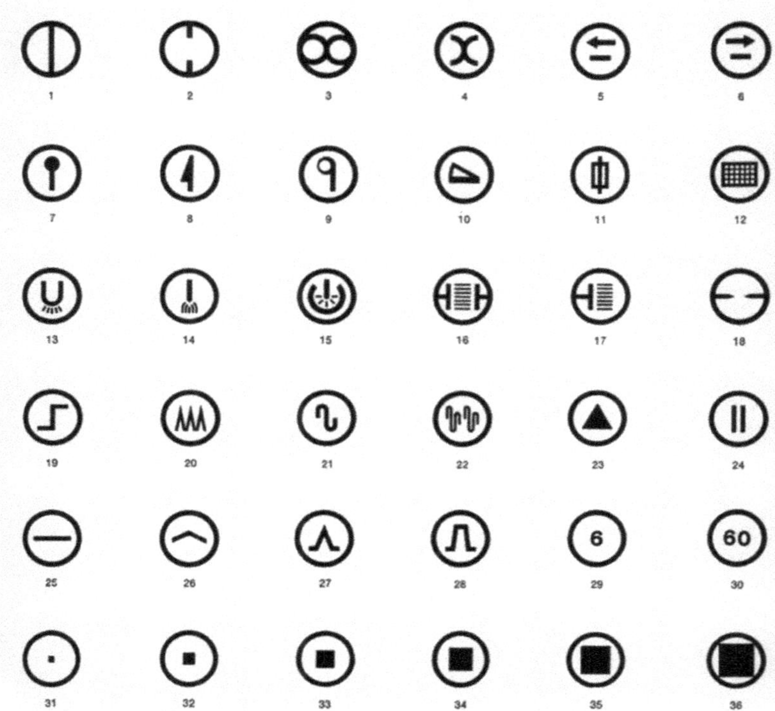

1) on 2) off 3) automatic 4) by hand 5) minus pole left 6) minus pole right 7) coagulation 8) cutting 9) resection 10) pedal switch 11) fuse element 12) neutral electrode 13) caustic 14) fulguration 15) endoscopy 16) two probes radiating 17) one probe radiating 18) spark gap regulation 19) galvanic current 20) faradic current 21) current from tube 22) current from spark gap 23) interference, danger 24) resonance 25) current, constant 26) current, increasing 27) triangle current 28) trapezoid current 29-30) 31-36) quantitative radiation measure

Sign System for Electro Medical Instruments, 1964
Tomas Maldonado & Gui Bonsiepe

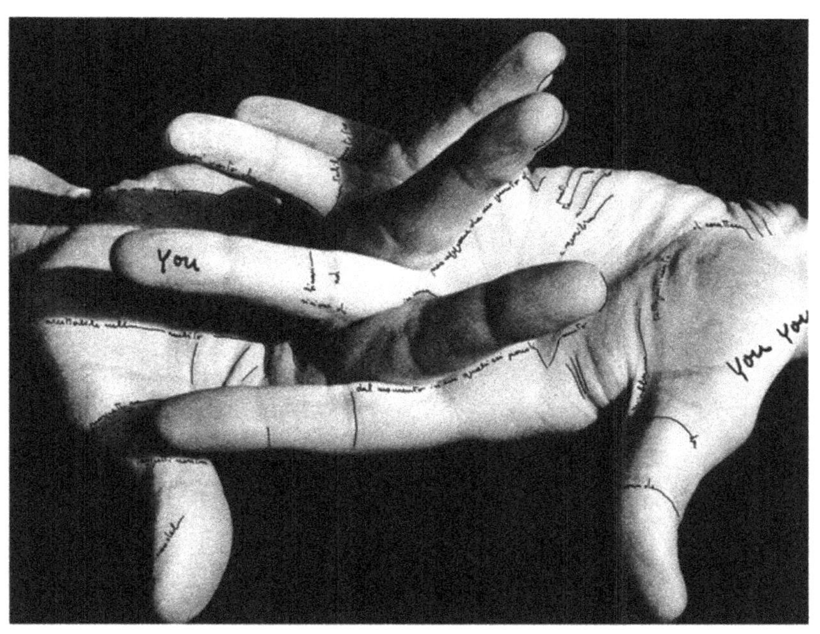

Le mie parole (My Words), 1973
Ketty La Rocca
Drawing on photograph, 24 x 30 cm.
Courtesy Sammlung P., Wien and Kadel Willborn, Düsseldorf.

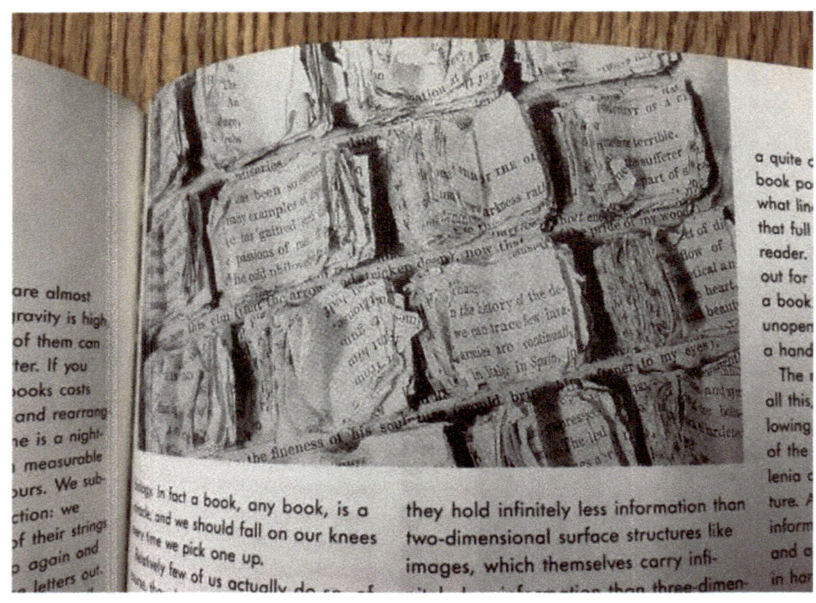

1117; Geysers and how they are explained, 1986
Andrew Masullo
Photograph of a detail. Collection of Doris Ammann, Zurich.

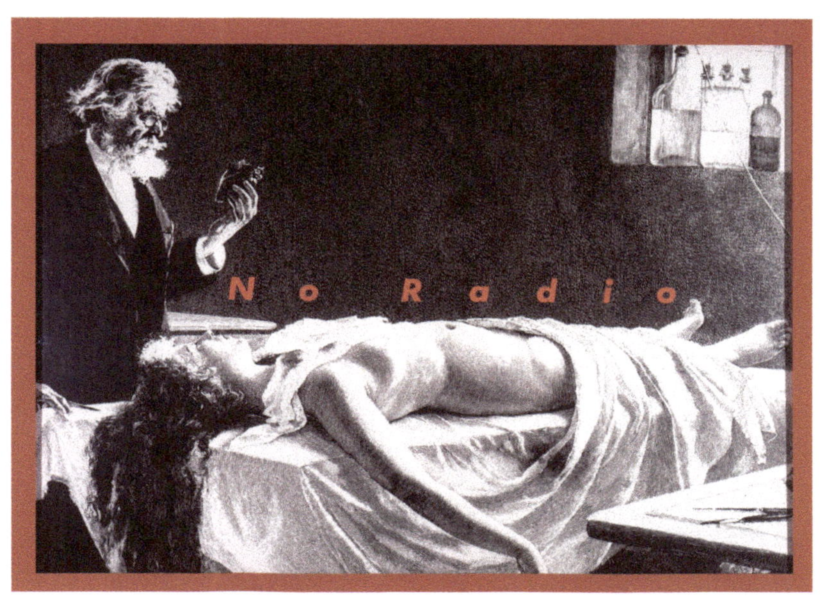

Untitled (No Radio), 1988
Barbara Kruger
Photograph 51 ½" by 68 ½" © Barbara Kruger.
Courtesy Mary Boone Gallery, New York (MBG#4781).

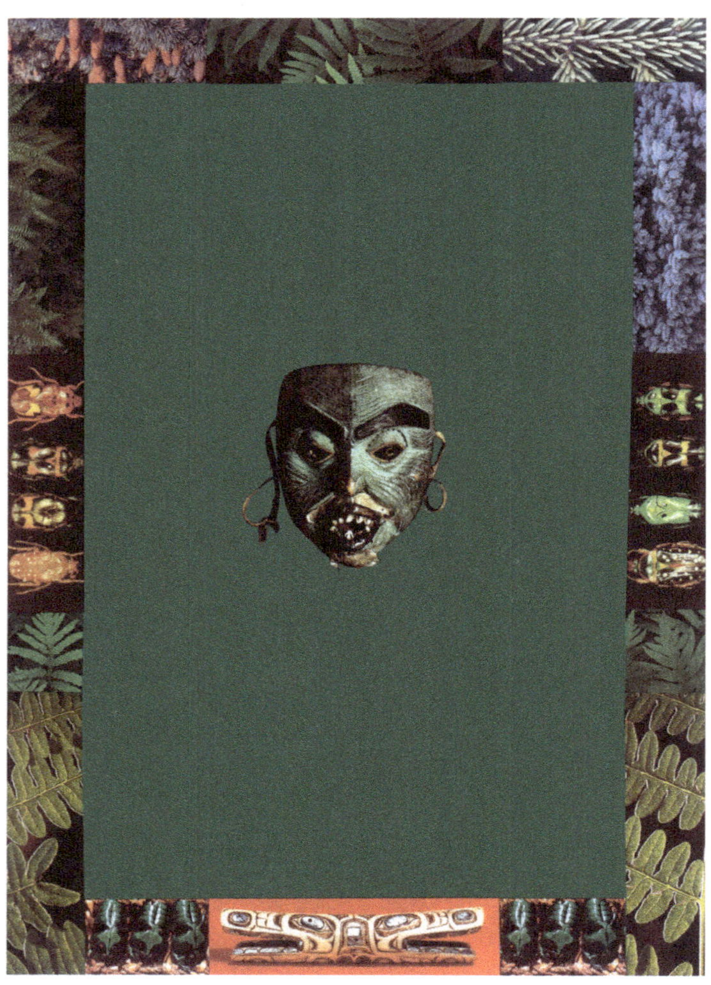

Green Mask, 1986
Sarah Charlesworth
Cibachrome with lacquered wood frame.

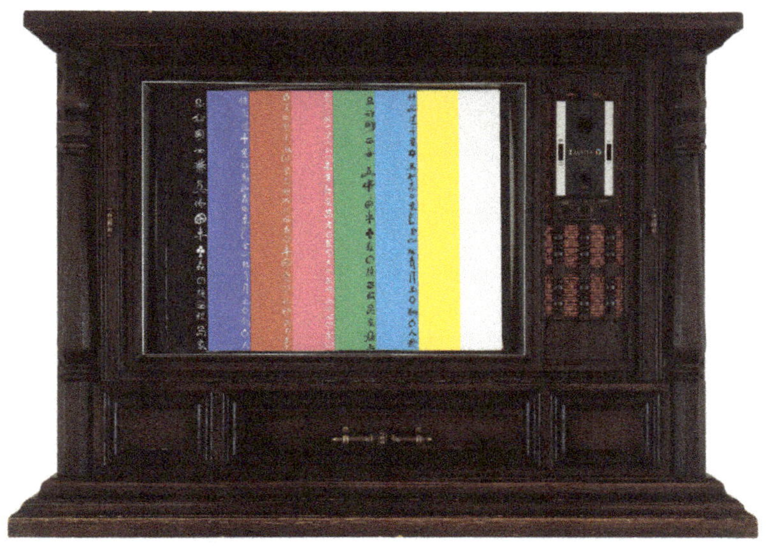

Rosetta Stone, Channel 10, 1983
Nam June Paik
Oil on canvas and TV facing 31 x 42 1/2 x 6 1/4"
JPMorgan Chase Art Collection © Nam June Paik Estate; Courtesy Gagosian.

ON DISCOVERY VI

Artforum
March
1989

§ Some people speak with fluidity (which does not necessarily imply that they speak correctly). Nobody counts with fluidity (although one may do so correctly). The reason is that numbers are clear and distinct. There are definite intervals that must be between numbers for them to be understood. The alphanumerical code, then (the signs of which are inscribed on the keyboard of typewriters), is a collage of fluency with stuttering. The letters (which are meant to render spoken sounds visual) merge to form words, the words merge to form sentences, and the sentences merge to form a discourse; but the numbers cluster in mosaic patterns called "algorithms." Still, typewriters handle letters as if they were numbers. A separate key moves each letter. Typewriters do not write fluently, but they "process" the letters. In fact: they are not writers but counters. Let us consider why this is so. § There is an easy explanation: all mechanisms stutter — even if they seem to be gliding. (All one has to do is observe a badly working motor car or film projector to confirm this.) But the easy explanation begs the question, which is really: "*Why* do all mechanisms, including typewriters, stutter?" Here is the answer: because everything stutters. Of course, just as you have to listen very carefully to hear that someone who speaks fluently stutters, you have to look very closely, sometimes with highly specialised and sensitised equipment, to discern this stuttering in all the world's mechanisms and operations. Thus it was only recently that Max Planck, generally regarded as the father of the quantum theory of modern physics, was able to show how oscillating atoms absorb and emit energy in quanta, rather than in the continuous flow posited by classical physics. Planck's work then, in simple terms, was the first to demonstrate that everything stutters (is "quantic"), although as early as Democritus some people suspected that this was so. Planck's work implies that clear and distinct (stuttering) numbers are adequate to the world, and that fluent letters cannot grasp it. That is, that the world is indescribable but that it can be counted. This is why numbers should leave the alphanumerical code, become independent of it. This, in fact, is already happening: we have already begun to establish new codes (like the digital one) to feed computers. As for letters — if they want to survive — they have to simulate numbers. And this is why typewriters stutter. However, a few remarks are in order. For instance: in order to count, you have to divide any given thing into little bits ("calculi"), and stick a number on each bit. Thus it may be held that the notion that the world consists of countable particles may be a consequence of our counting. In other words, it may not be a discovery at all, but an invention: the world may be counted perhaps because we have ourselves handled it that way. Thus it may not be true that the number code is adequate for the world, but that we have made the world adequate to numbers. This is discomfiting. § Because this is the case, we have to suppose that the world was structured differently before this. Ever since the time of the Greek philosophers, people used letters to describe the world. Thus one could assume that the world was once structured according to the rules of disciplined discourse, which are the rules of logic, and not, as is the case now, according to the rules of disciplined counting, which are the rules of mathematics. In fact, as late as Hegel, it was held that everything in the world is logical (which to us is an insane proposition). But if we can attribute Hegel's "insanity" to the fact that he was a writer, we may have to attribute our own "insanity" to the fact that we are the users of computers, which "tell" us that everything in the world is an absurd accident the probability of which may be calculated. § The situation becomes even more uncomfortable when we consider Russell and Whitehead. They demonstrated in *Principia Mathematica* that the rules of logic cannot be fully reduced to the rules of mathematics. When they attempted to handle logical discourse according to mathematical rules ("proposition calculus"), they found a fundamental discrepancy between the two structures. Thus we can build no satisfactory bridge between the Hegelian and the Planckian world. In short, ever since we began to count methodically (ever since Descartes proposed analytical geometry), the structure of the world has changed, and it cannot be satisfactorily tied to its previous structure. And it is this disquieting fact that we must try to face at present. § We may try to argue that it is we ourselves who decide the structure of the world. If we like to write, the world will follow the structure of logical discourse, and if we prefer to count, it will follow the structure of mathematics and will become a particle swarm. But unfortunately such an argument will not hold up. For it is only after we began to count that we could have machines (for instance typewriters), and we cannot live without machines, even if we wanted to. Therefore we cannot but count the world. § At this point, we court the danger of falling into the bottomless pit of religious exaltation. To avoid the risk of Pythagorean worship of numbers, we should compare the gesture of writing with the gesture of counting. If you write by hand, you draw a complex and partially interrupted line from left to right (that is: if you live in the Western world). Yours is a linear gesture. If you count, you pick pebbles. Yours is a point-like gesture. But when you count, first you pick (you

calculate "I plus I"), and then you assemble (you compute "2"); in other words, you analyse and then you synthesise. This is the radical difference between writing and counting: to count is to aim at a synthesis, while writing is only critical (analytic).
§ Some people who are committed to writing try to deny this. They identify counting only with calculating, and say that it is a cold, unfeeling activity. This is malevolent misunderstanding. One who calculates does so in order to compute something new, something that has not previously existed. The creative heat in counting is inaccessible to those who have not learned how to handle numbers. They cannot perceive the philosophical beauty and depth of some equations (like Einstein's). But now computers can transcode the numbers into shapes, sounds, and colours, and thus the beauty and depth of counting can be perceived by our senses. The creative power of counting can now be seen with one's eyes on computer screens, heard with one's ears in synthesised music, and soon may well be graspable with one's hands in holograms. This is what is so

fascinating about counting: that it is now capable of projecting worlds that can be perceived by our senses. § Those who vilify counting insist that those projected worlds are nothing but fictitious simulations of the true world. Perhaps they are right, but for the wrong reasons. For those projected worlds are computations of calculations, but so is our "true" world, as our nervous system receives point-like stimuli that our brain computes into our perceptions of the world. Thus, either the projected worlds are just as true as the true one, or the true world is just as fictitious as the projected worlds. The marvellous thing about counting is that as it enables us to project alternative worlds, we need no longer be subject to a single one. § "Ah Love! Could you and I with Fate conspire/ To grasp this sorry Scheme of Things entire,/ Would not we shatter it to bits — and then/ Re-mould it nearer to the Heart's Desire!," wrote Omar Khayyam in the *Rubaiyat*. Those who claim that we are about to shatter to bits that sorry scheme of things entire are perhaps unable to see that we may be able to compute it nearer to the heart's desire. It is time for those people to learn how to count. *

ON FUTURE ARCHITECTURE

Artforum
April
1989

§ Humans inhabit — nests, caves, tents, houses, or cubes piled one on top of another. One might even say that the act of inhabiting is inevitable because people *need* habit, because experience only becomes meaningful to us through habitual repetition. Theory of information tells us, for example, that it is only through repetition that a "noise" becomes information. Knowledge of information theory, however, is not required to understand that a wanderer who has no habitat will process information differently from those of us who have permanent homes. Medieval thinkers believed that we were all such aimless tourists, *homines viatores*; that we had lost our heavenly home and must roam erratically through this valley of tears called "the world." For this reason, Maimonides wrote his *Guide to the Perplexed* in the 12th century. Today, we have our *Guides Michelin* when we leave our homes. And yet still we feel unsheltered, exposed, vulnerable. Perhaps this is because our houses are no longer habitable, and we need to look critically at our homes. § A house has been, traditionally, a roof and four walls. The roof is a shield, designed to protect the inhabitants from whatever is above, from what is superior, be it Nature or a Superior Being. Those who hide under the roof are subjects of (and subject to) superior forces, and hope that those forces, be they hail or commandments, will not find them. The builder of roofs, the architect, used to be the most important of all the artists. But we no longer believe in superior forces. We are sovereign people, nobody's subjects, and therefore no longer need such an artist. A wall also protects the inhabitant from what is outside. It has two sides: the outside faces the "dangerous foreigner" who threatens to invade; the inside faces the indigenous native. The Berlin wall shows how this dual system works: the outside is political, the inside keeps a secret. But we are no longer convinced that the danger is outside, and, further, we do not like to be imprisoned within secrets. We tend to believe that all walls should go down. § But even those of us who still believe in keeping secrets (and in being kept) cannot help but make holes in walls – doors and windows – because even patriots like to take a stroll and look out at what happens. Windows provide vistas; through them we see the outside from the inside. The Greeks called such a vision *theoria*: you need not get wet while looking. But we are no longer convinced that such an uncommitted, "pure" vision provides knowledge. Windows are no longer useful. Doors permit exits and entrances. One goes out through the door to conquer the world, and loses oneself there; one comes back through the door to find oneself, and loses the world. Hegel called this pendular motion the "unhappy conscience." More problematically, the police (government bureaucracy) may enter through the door, and burglars (private interests) through the window. Doors are not happy inventions.

§ All in all, in fact, the house as we know it is not a very successful idea – maybe that is why the house consisting of a roof and four walls belongs only in fairytales by now. For the global shakeup referred to as the "communications revolution" has reduced that actual structure to ruins. Material and immaterial cables have penetrated it, have made Swiss cheese of it: antennae through the roof, television through the walls, telephones between individual houses. We no longer dwell, but hide in ruins through which blow the blizzards of communication. No use trying to adapt those ruins: a new architecture for people who "survive the revolution" is called for. § To begin, we must relinquish geographical for topological thinking. We can no longer think of a house that is placed somewhere geographically, for instance on a hill near a river. This will not be easy (consider how difficult it was to rethink geography from a plane to the surface of a volume). But we must try, and computer generated images may help us. Take the solar system as an example. We used to think of Earth as occupying a place within that system. Computer-generated images now demonstrate that Earth is a curve within a wire net called "the gravitational field of the Sun." We could imagine a house as a curve within the wire net called "human relations." Within that curve, human relations become ever denser, and the house is that point where the relations are densest. § The new house should be "attractive" (in the sense in which Earth is attractive). It should attract ever-new human relations. It must be in a constant process of construction. Ever-new relations must be its input, and it must process them into information. That information must be transmitted to other houses. The house must become a knot within the human network, a creative knot within which the sum of information at the disposal of humanity (the sum of "culture") increases — which is to say that it must be a knot built on material and immaterial cables. § This is a dangerous architectural project, for we now know only two forms of connecting cables: nets (example: telephones), or bundles (example: television). If the new house were to be part of a bundle (in Latin, *fasces*), it would become a support for an as-yet-unimaginable form of totalitarianism. All the houses would then produce or dispose of the same information (in Nazi Germany this was called *Gleichschaltung*, political coordination and the elimination of opponents). Future architects must take care to avoid such bundling, and to provide for a "dialogical network." This is a technical problem. Architects (being technicians and artists) are competent to solve it. § But there is a greater nontechnical — existential — danger. People who inhabit such houses will have nowhere to hide (no roof, no wall); they will have nothing to cling to. They can do nothing but reach out their hands and try to hold onto the hands of other people. And thus, hand in hand, face the void without any guarantee that they will not be swallowed up in it. We must accept that danger, because the alternative is even more dangerous: to go on hiding within the ruins of houses become uninhabitable, or to roam about in motor cars. We must either risk the dangers in becoming upright creators within the void, or continue to settle for the limits of being perpetual squatters. *

† *This essay was republished in Artforum in May 1990 as "On Future Architecture II."*

WONDERING ABOUT SCIENCE

Artforum
Summer
1989

§ In one sense, the purpose of science is to do away with wonders: science is a discourse of explanation, and one definition of a "wonder" is a thing not yet explained. Science is said to enlighten us because it allows us to understand and master phenomena, instead of wondering about them. Thus, as scientific knowledge advances, the world grows less and less "wonder-full," and more and more wonder-empty. § On the other hand, however, our feeling of wonder deepens as science develops. Science cannot explain everything — it cannot erase wonders from our consciousness, but must content itself with pushing their boundaries ever farther into the background. Our feeling of wonder follows this progress toward the abyss, and as the world, and we within it, grows ever more wonder-empty, we are ever more bewildered. The less wonderful the world is, the more we wonder why it is there — and even, indeed, if it *is* there. Like Martin Heidegger, we ask questions like: Why is there anything when there could be nothing? § In yet another sense, science may be said to be actually producing wonders. For the unexpected thing, the thing that is improbable and surprising, is also a wonder, and this is the sort of event that scientific knowledge, applied through technology to animate and inanimate nature, can produce. § Before entering this labyrinth, a word of caution: the word "wonder" is doubly ambiguous. It may describe the cause of an emotion or it may describe the emotion itself, and if it refers to an emotion, this too is bivalent, "to wonder at" or "to wonder if." The words "miracle" and "marvel," Latinate equivalents of the Germanic word "wonder" (it is the disposition in English of Latin and German equivalents, by the way, that makes the language so subtle), stem from the verb *mirari*, which we recognise in other terms such as "mirror" and "admiration." They are no clearer than the Germanic "wonder," but they provide the concept with yet further connotations. The latter of the two words in particular may prove helpful to us here. § Aristotle held that philosophy (and thus science) is brought about through admiration: *propter admirationem enim.*

"Admiration" in this context is a strong word, meaning the feeling we get in that fleeting moment when we face something we had not expected. There are two elements in this kind of admiration: awe and doubt. Characteristically, the modern tradition stresses the element of doubt as the source of philosophy, and doubt is indeed a strong experience. One that can bring into question the very foundations of our sense of the world, and of ourselves. But awe is even stronger: it can leave us speechless. (This may be why the modern tradition, a demystifying, sceptical tradition, is uneasy with awe – it loves words.) The ancients, more familiar with the doubleness of admiration, knew that philosophy and science are not only doubtful but also awful. We "post-Moderns" are relearning the lesson. As science advances, both erasing and creating one wonder after another, it shows again how doubtful and awful it itself is.
§ Aristotle was surely right in attributing philosophy to admiration: people never in awe – "blasé" people – will produce no science, and neither will those who never doubt, who accept wonders as mysteries not

to be questioned: Still, we no longer quite share Aristotle's experience of admiration. We have a different sense of the unexpected. The meaning of "wonder" has shifted, if one were to write a history of Western civilisation based on such shifts in the word's meaning, it might look like this: In the first, protohistorical stage, the world and the people within it were experienced and understood as obeying a circular order. Day was followed by night and night by day, summer by fall by winter by spring by summer, birth by death and death by rebirth. That circular order, however, was open to intervention from outside: the sun might suddenly standstill, floods or fire might interrupt the cycle of the seasons, a person might die and be resurrected in the same body instead of being reborn in a new one. Although such interventions were rare, and were surely considered wonderful, they were not unexpected, not, at least, in the sense of inciting what Aristotle would later call "admiration." They had their place in the world and in human life. Manifestations ("hierophanies") of what transcended the world, they might provoke awe, but they could not be doubted: they were decipherable messages from the greater powers of existence. It was precisely these interruptions of order that gave the world and the life within it their meanings. § Then, people on the Ionian coast began to "admire" these interruptions. Faced with the unexpected, they were struck with awe and doubt, and instead of deciphering it, they began to wonder about it, to ask questions about it. Philosophy, and later science, were born. The result was that we began to understand ourselves and the world differently. The circular order came to be seen as somehow beneath the surface of the world; the cycle of the days, of the seasons, and so forth — everything we perceive — was taken as merely an appearance of a hidden, fundamental order, the *mathesis universalis*. And the apparent interruptions or irregularities in the cycle, which had thus far been taken as wonders, could now be explained by recourse to that fundamental ("real") order. The planets seemed to move erratically, for instance, but "in reality" they followed circular orbits, or epicycles, that themselves sat on larger circular orbits. Thus appearances could be "saved." It followed that it was not the irregular events in the passage of things that were wonderful, but the fundamental circular harmony itself; not the interruptions of order that gave the world meaning, but the order's own pattern. § In Northern Italy during the 15th century, people began to admire the circular planetary order, which struck them as entirely improbable and unexpected. They began to wonder about it, to ask questions about it — questions that the Ptolemaic system could not answer. But they found that appearances could once again be "saved" by recourse to the Copernican system, which was simpler, and satisfied more of their doubts. And they also found something even more wonderful: new, alternative orders that could be devised within other new systems might be used not only to "save" appearances, but also to manipulate them — to produce wonders. The new orders, or "theories," could be practically applied to bring about improbable situations. Modern science was born, and, later, modern technology. And it was no longer the world's fundamental harmony that was wonderful, but the fact that we could manipulate the world and use it for wonder production. The knowledge that we had that power constituted a radical humanism. It transferred wonder from exterior events into our innermost selves: we ourselves became wonderful. § We are entering a new stage in this shifting meaning of wonder: we are beginning to admire our ability to produce wonders. That faculty strikes us with awe and doubt, because it is so improbable and unexpected. We begin to ask questions about ourselves, to wonder about ourselves, to "analyse" what is "within us." And we discover something really astounding: there is nothing within us, there is no consistent core, no "self," no "I," only a swarm of pointlike recombinant virtualities in a constant state of flux. And these virtualities may not be unique to us, or even to animals: our thoughts can be analysed into algorithms and projected through computers, the responsibility for our decisions is already being shared with the computer by virtue of its ability to process vast quantities of information, and in the near future our desires, wishes, and even our sense of the power we have to create wonders may be passed on to our machines. The discovery that we are not really wonderful or marvellous does not really astound us, however: we suspected it all along. What does astound us is the fact that despite our wonder-emptiness, an ever-increasing quantity of wonders is being produced "through us." And this makes our sense of wonder bottomless. § This short outline of the history of Western civilisation (which is itself both doubtful and awful) should not be read as a series of successive phases. The stages overlap, and all remain present with us. Even now, we would fall on our knees if the sun were all of a sudden to stand still. Immediately afterward, though, we would devise astronomical, optical, and psychological explanations to show that the event was no wonder but something we could have predicted. Even now, we cannot but be astounded by the symbiotic orderliness of life on Earth, with each species in its own ecological niche, and each organism equipped with its appropriate organs, immediately afterward, though, we begin to say that this order is as violent as it is harmonious, and that in any case it is the result of blind chance, and could just as easily have been quite different. Even now, in other words, we retain the protohistorical and the Aristotelian meanings of wonder, along with the contemporary one. § Still, all previous meanings of the word pale compared to the sense of wonder taking hold of us right now. We know that there is nothing wonderful about the world, or about ourselves (and nothing to be admired), and still we produce wonder after wonder. Perhaps we have decided that what science is really about is not to explain wonders (there are none to be explained) but to create them. And this is the source of endless wonder. § At the present stage of scientific progress, this is more or less how we understand the world and ourselves within it: a particulate cloud of gas and dust expands after an initial explosion. The cloud is thinly spread – full of holes, of "nothingness" – and as it expands, it grows ever thinner, ever more "nothing." Here and there, however, clusters of particles have formed, as if in opposition to the general tendency toward thinner distribution – and as if in opposition to the second law of thermodynamics. This opposition is only apparent and temporary: the accidents of conglomeration are statistically "necessary," and as the general expansion goes on, entropy will demand that the clusters eventually dissolve. We may call the particles "energy" and the clusters "matter" if we keep in mind that these terms are relative to each other, for "matter" is closely packed energy and "energy" is loosely distributed matter. The pattern followed by the spreading cloud can be plotted as overlapping fields of particles, clusters, and emptiness. We shall then find that we ourselves are clusters wherein several fields intermingle. § We can visualise this understanding of ourselves and of the universe by imagining that we can feed all the algorithms responsible for it (Einstein's relativity equation, and so forth) into a computer. Wirelike nets will appear on the computer screen to show the patterns of the fields. Here and there, the nets will interfere with each other, forming baglike protuberances. One such protuberance may be identified as showing the planet Earth, another, more complex one, as the biomass that covers Earth; and yet another, even more complex one as ourselves within that biomass. If we "animate" the image, we may watch these protuberances form and complexify. Then, gradually, they will grow shallower, until finally they fade back into the regular grid of the nets. The spectacle will end when all the net's irregularities have disappeared without trace, when the pattern stretches uniformly (without form) in every direction. If we feel like it, we may call this happy (or unhappy) end of our computer-generated video "thermic death."

§ Watching this video, we may be struck by the idea that everything we are used to calling "matter" is a wonder. As the product of an accidental cohesion or collision of particles in a field whose tendency is to disperse rather than to coalesce, it is per se improbable and unexpected. It follows that the more complex matter is, the more it is wonderful, because the more improbable are the collisions that create it. A hydrogen atom, produced by the collision of only two particles, is less wonderful than a complex chain of molecules, and that chain is less wonderful than is our own nervous system. This idea is curious for two reasons: first, the term "wonder" may now be quantified, and second, we can produce wonders by forcing particles to collide. And today we can actually do this. We can compute particle collisions; can produce "artificial" matter — we call the process "fusion."

§ But this curious idea begs an even more curious question. If "we" are an ephemeral protuberance of overlapping fields, how can we compute other protuberances? This question has many answers, but only one that agrees with the computer-generated video: we are the result of highly improbable but statistically calculable coincidences, and by this coincidence we are capable of generating further coincidences. To put this more traditionally, the species *Homo sapiens,* an accidental, improbable product of chance, accidentally has the ability to produce further improbable situations by its own intention. In the human species, in other words, chance accidentally turns around and becomes intention. This proposition articulates a very deep sense of wonder: it is much more wonderful, more doubtful and awful, than those answers that contain such apparently wonderful but actually spurious terms as "mind" and "spirit." § Let us face it with courage: science has now reached a point at which it can produce any amount of wonders, on any level. One of these levels, we have seen, is the manipulation of particles to collide, and through this fusion process we can produce "plasma," a material having some of the properties of energy and some of the properties of matter. In making plasma we are imitating what happened accidentally in nature (and continues to happen in the centre of the Sun). In fact, we are imitating what can be called "the origin of the material world"; if you prefer, we are imitating the Creator. And we can do the same thing in any number of other ways. In the production of "artificial" chemical elements, for example, we are already exceeding what happened accidentally in nature — we are improving upon the Creation. Similarly, the "artificial" molecules we now can make are not so much replications of pre-existing molecules as additions to the world's variety. The "artificial" polymers we can create may eventually lead to "artificial" alternative life forms. And we are only starting. By computing the elements of existing genetic information, we can produce alternative plants and animals, and we can do so according to a deliberate program, not according to nature's blind chance. By computing the elements of what used to be called "the mind," we can produce "artificial" intelligences, with "artificial" thoughts, feelings, wishes, and actions. Nothing seems to stand in the way of our reaching levels of wonder never attained in nature. These levels may defy our imagination, but not the competence of science. If by "wonder" we understand improbable clusters of particles, there is no limit to the wonders science may eventually produce. § But this is precisely not what we mean by "wonder" when we say that a new sense of wonder is taking hold of us today. This new sense of wonder (if indeed it is new) makes us ask: If every wonder, whether natural or artificial, is condemned to disappear within the general tendency toward probability (toward entropy), why make them? If every unexpected, improbable event, be it the product of blind chance or of human deliberation, is finally to be forgotten, why deliberate it? Because the ultimate wonder, the mystery of all mysteries, is not the improbable marvel that every existing thing can claim to be called, but the fact that all these marvels are in the end wonder-empty. § As we try to formulate this new sense of wonder, it slips between our fingers. Wonder today is attached to the turning of chance into deliberation that we feel happens "within" us, or "through" us — or, even more radically, that we feel the "self" *is*. If we fed the algorithm for this sense of wonder into our computer, we might see the protuberances that meant "us" become a series of vortices swirling on the screen, and spouting yet further irregularities into the net-spouting wonders. This swirling, which defines the difference between chance and deliberation, constitutes an acceleration of accidents: if the world were given enough time, the products of contemporary science could come about by chance, by a highly improbable "natural" collision of particles, instead of through human deliberation. Thus we can understand deliberation as the production of effects very much earlier than nature does. Yet to say that deliberation is an acceleration of chance is only to transfer our sense of wonder: what is this acceleration?

§ One point, however, remains: whatever "chance" and "deliberation" may mean; they both deny law and order. They deny law both in the sense of "natural law" and in the sense of "transcendental program"; and they deny order both in the sense of "underlying harmony" and in the sense of "logical and mathematical order." If there is chance and deliberation, there can be no law and order. The Greek term for "law and order" is *norm*; if there is no norm, nothing is normal, and everything is "e-normous." Which is to say that everything is a wonder. And if everything is a wonder, nothing is, because there is then no distinction between wonder and not-wonder. Furthermore, the fact that there is no law and order is in itself enormous. And it is this enormity that is the source of our sense of wonder. § In the face of all this, two answers are open to us. The first: once we have discovered that there is nothing wonderful about the world and about ourselves, that it is all a blind game of chance that we, mysteriously, can accelerate, and that will automatically exhaust itself in time, we can play at it for the pure fun of it. We can produce wonders a little more intelligent than the idiotic wonder of nature (of which we ourselves are a good example): a little more intelligent atoms, molecules, living organisms, and human beings. This is the answer given by *Homo ludens*, the aesthetic, artistic response. § The other answer: once we have discovered that the world and life within it are absurd (wonder-empty), we must face this enormity by going it one better. Everything we do is an absurd gesture in the face of the absurdity of life and death, so let us be honest about it — let us be deliberately absurd. Let us admit that science and technology are absurd gestures, that "artificial" wonders are absurd wonders, and let us make these gestures and produce these wonders precisely because they are absurd. This is a familiar answer, aphorised long ago as *credo quia absurdum*: I believe it because it is absurd. This is the answer given by *Homo religiosus*. § None of these answers is satisfactory: none quells our wondering. But then maybe nothing will — which is why it is called "wonder." *

ON AN UNSPEAKABLE FUTURE

Artforum
March
1990

§ Wittgenstein's *Tractatus Logico Philosophicus* concludes with the statement, "Whatever cannot be spoken about must be silenced." A few paragraphs earlier Wittgenstein writes, "It is true that some matters are unspeakable. These *show*, they are what is mystical." (I have translated these statements from the German to suit my purpose.) I want to suggest that these ideas are wrong, and that we have to show them to be wrong if we are to understand what is going on right now. For an increasing body of thought that cannot be put into words may now be expressed in other ways, without anything mystical attached: we are simply learning to use a new type of image to express the thoughts we have that fall into those regions where words fail us. § An early example of this is the nuclear physicist's use of signs that mean atom particles. These signs can be considered images of concepts — "ideograms." We may invent words for them — the word *quark*, for instance — but to use these words is to speak not so much about the concepts of particle atomics as about the signs that mean those concepts. To grasp the concepts demands learning the signs, and the rules by which they are processed. To talk about them in language is to end up asking questions like, "Are quarks real or are they fictions?" and these are meaningless questions. The concepts, then, are strictly unspeakable. Yet there is obviously nothing mystical about them; they can be submitted to observation and experiment, and may have practical applications in technology. § Apparently complex phenomena may often be reduced to simple structures. Over time, for instance, stones on a mountainside may gradually drift downhill, as if of their own will, but this unpredictable motion can be explained simply as a consequence of the law of gravity. Other phenomena, though, cannot be so reduced, keeping the same degree of complexity however we want to analyse them. The line between sea and shore, whether of a continent or of a tiny island, is as complex on the scale of miles as it is on the scale of millimetres. The same is true of meteorological phenomena, and, in the end, of most of the phenomena of

the objective world — including the slow downward movement of stones on a hillside. Today we have found a way to express such phenomena in mathematical equations, and these equations may be fed into computers and shown on video screens as images.
§ We can invent words to speak about these images, like the word *fractal,* or the words *Mandelbrot monster.* But such terms refer only to the equations and to the pictures; they cannot convey the concepts that the equations and pictures convey. If we want to get at those concepts, we have to learn the mathematical and computer codes. If not, we end up asking questions like "Does this fractal image look like the Alps because the Alps too have a fractal structure, or because fractal images are able to simulate the structure of the Alps?" Such questions are meaningless. And there is nothing mystical about a fractal image. If it looks like nothing at all, it does so not because it means some mysterious sublime, but because it means an equation. § What is happening is that our concepts have advanced beyond the scope of verbal language and we are inventing ever more refined codes to

articulate them. In the *Mandelbrot monster*, these codes are pictorial, and they challenge us to develop a fresh kind of conceptual imagination, as different from verbal thought as mathematical thinking is. Such an imagination would enable us to conceive of a world (and our position therein) that we are incapable of conceiving through speech. This is a formidable challenge, demanding not only that we replace philosophy (a "logical," verbal discourse) with another pictorial method of reflection but also that we sever the link between word and concept that has dominated our thinking ever since the invention of alphabetic writing. § The alphabet's visual encoding of spoken language (letters are visual signs for phonemes) has proved a powerful tool: over history, much of our disciplined conceptual thinking has been encoded in writing. Despite our various visual traditions, I would argue that ours is a logocentric culture (for Heidegger, the word is "the dwelling of Being"), which cherishes the belief that if an idea cannot be expressed verbally it must necessarily be muddled, if, indeed, it merits being called an idea at all. And we have amplified the competence of language in poetry and philosophy, also powerful tools. It is due to these that our languages have expanded like gases into the void, and that they have become such refined, exact, beautiful instruments not only for thinking but also for feeling.

§ But let us be honest about this: verbal languages have never had total hold upon our thinking. We have always felt that their competence is limited, their universe of meanings finite. The inadequacy of speech is an old theme in Western philosophy and literature, and has been sensed by many visual artists. Mathematicians too have for centuries found equations more articulate in their field than words. (Try finding words to express $\sqrt{2}$.) We know that some of our concepts are expressed better in numbers than verbally, and that the objective world demands to be counted as much as to be discussed. This is why our code of writing is called "alphanumerical," containing both letters and numerals.

§ It is true that numbers have often seemed somehow coidentical with letters, not so much ideograms (image for concepts) as a convenient shorthand — 103 instead of a hundred and three. In fact we used to believe that mathematics, the rules of numbers, could be reduced to logic, the rules of letters. It has been shown, however, that this is not so (*Principia Mathematica*, by Bertrand Russell and Alfred North Whitehead) — that thinking in numbers is quite different from thinking in speech. What is happening now is that numbers are leaving the alphanumerical code to branch off into new codes (for example, the digital code), and that an increasing amount of our thinking is being articulated in those new codes and in the images they produce. In an important sense, we are beginning to emancipate ourselves from word languages, and are beginning to exercise a new imagination. § This new imagination may even now be observed in the form of a new type of image. Some of these images are produced by people we might call "artists," but most are made by people we would be more likely to tall "scientists," or "computer programmers." We need to put such categories aside to understand the newly emerging imagination.

We should instead distinguish between two types of images: those traditional images that imagine situations — loosely speaking, "images of the world" — and those computer visions that imagine thoughts, or "images of thinking." These categories may overlap: pictures from the past will reveal some of the thinking of those who produced them (religious ideas, for instance, in Byzantine mosaics), and in some fractal images we may decipher, say, formations like the Alps. But this overlap should not confuse us, for the intentions behind these two types of pictures are in fact quite different. The first intention is to publish a personal vision; the second is to express a thought that cannot be expressed in the words of a language. The first type of image wants to be spoken about in order to conceive its meaning. The other type cannot be spoken about because its meaning is beyond words. § If we put aside our traditional ideas of pictures, we may begin to grasp what it is that is happening at present. Art, in a new sense of that term, is beginning, in a new way, to absorb scientific and philosophical discourse, and thus to articulate our most abstract and refined concepts of the world and of our position within it. It is too early to try to define what art may mean in the future, and were we to try, this itself might prove to be a concept that defied verbal definition. But it may well be that to grasp the new concept of art we will have to look at those new pictures. And one thing may certainly be said at this early stage: those new pictures, and the new imagination they express, is opening up an unspeakable future for us. *

ON POPES

Artforum
October
1990

§ Art criticism, as an attempt to translate from images into the words of a language, has to do with the building of bridges. In ancient Rome, bridge builders were called *pontifices*, and the head builder — *pontifex maximus* — still lives in that city. Which is to say that art critics and the pope are in the same business. § Bridge building in general is an address of the problem of transportation over the abyss. The ancients, for example, thought there were two worlds, the mundane one below the Moon and the heavenly one above it, and a divide separated them. But traffic between the two worlds was essential if life was to have meaning. Bridge builders — pontiffs — were needed: They built a temple on a hill, called the "Capitol," that bridged the space between the sacred and the lowly political space called the "forum," and for most of the history of Western civilisation this bridge and its descendants carried the traffic between Heaven and Earth. Then came Sir Isaac Newton, who unified celestial and terrestrial mechanics, levelled Heaven to the ground, and did away with the abyss above the Moon, making bridges and pontiffs redundant. It took a while before people realised that this was what he had done. Now, however, it has become more or less obvious that though the hill (for instance the Capitol in Washington, D.C.) might claim some godlike authority over the plain (for instance *Art-"forum"* in New York), its priesthood is distinctly to this side of the divine. § Now suppose you want to translate the German expression *es gibt* into English. There are bridges called "dictionaries" that may lead you to the literal translation "it gives," but here the pontiffs have misled you. For a reason not immediately obvious, the correct translation is "there is," and to get at it you have to jump over the abyss that separates German from English. It is this jump that is called a "translation." This is not to say that dictionaries are useless. There are regions where German and English overlap, and dictionaries are good guides to them. But the expressions *es gibt* and "there is" seem to stand outside those regions, somewhere near the centres of the two universes of German and English, and these centres are separated by an abyss. It is here that pontiffs are needed. § This is true even with Newton, who seemed to have done away with the pontiffs between Heaven and Earth. Actually what Newton did was establish a grey zone where Heaven and Earth overlap, and he fixed the rules ordering that region. But eventually it became apparent that Newton's dictionary is sometimes misleading. There is a "big" universe that sits on top of or around the Newtonian one, where Einsteinian rules apply, and where astronauts take their ethereal strolls. And there is a "small" universe that sustains or sits inside the Newtonian one, and here Planckian rules apply, and govern atomic reactions. So Newton abolished one abyss only to end up leaving us with two. How are we to translate the concept "this table," an object whose behaviour remains largely explicable in Newtonian terms, into the macrocosmic and the microcosmic universe? By "curvature of space-time" upward, and by "probability wave" downward? This sounds as awkward as if we translated *es gibt* by "it gives," but we have to find accurate translations. Pontiffs are needed. § Let us imagine a pontifical artificial intelligence into which one feeds the words *es gibt* and gets back the words "there is." Then one feeds in "this table" and the pope spouts quantum mechanics. Let us go a step farther and feed in a picture postcard: the pope spouts a perfect description of it, in English, and with a smile. The same when one feeds in the Mona Lisa (in reproduction, of course). You might say that such artificially intelligent popes are an impossible nonsense. But we already have electronic intermixes; machines that translate light into sound and vice versa. Feed in an image of a sandwich and you hear the sandwich. Feed in a Schubert sonata and the machine translates it into an image. And we have computers into which you feed an algorithm and get back an image. Soon you will be able to get back a hologram as well. § Here art critics may shudder and artists may panic. If an artificially intelligent pope can translate sound into light and number into image, why shouldn't it translate light into sound, or rather into speech — from image to number to English? Wouldn't that be a kind of art criticism, and one as exact as quantum mechanics? Such intelligence would chew any sort of artwork into numbers, and then spit it out as text. Wouldn't that text be a quantified criticism of that art? And then all the critics would be out of work, and all the artists would be subject to relentless examination without any chance of appeal. Soon the artistic scene, the "art forum," would be translated into a desert. § This is not going to happen, however. Artificially intelligent popes can only build bridges in the gray zones where universes overlap, not where they are separated by abysses. They can only build bridges where bridges are unnecessary. A computer that would translate image to word would resemble the dictionary that would define *es gibt* as "it gives." For if you translate *es gibt* by "there is," you seem to be cognisant of a metalanguage that embraces German and English equally, for you have equal knowledge of both, across the abyss of their dissimilarity. And the bridge you build is made of that metalanguage. Similarly, if you translate "this table" from the Newtonian universe into the universe of quantum physics, you seem to be in a meta-universe that embraces both these universes, just as our artificially intelligent art critic seems to stand in a meta-universe embracing both images and words. But no such meta-universes exist. What is actually happening is something different: if you translate from German into English, German remains the meta-universe, and English becomes an object that can be lifted into it but can never be coidentical with it. And if you want to render "this table" in quantic equations, you have to lift the language of quantum mechanics into the meta-universe of English. In both these examples the process works both ways. Thus the "meta-" level is a reversible one, and if you were to build papal thrones on it, His Holiness would sit on slippery ground and would not be very comfortable. § This argument is important, for it means that art critics stand on the level of words, and that they try to lift images onto that level. But there is an abyss. Words are incompetent to utter the meanings of images, or of music, or of algorithms, or, for that matter, of the simplest gestures of the body. By the same token, images are incompetent to utter the meaning of a verbal language. There are abysses between the cultural codes, or, if you prefer, the cultural codes are islands of meaning afloat in an ocean of meaningless nothing. An art critic is a pontiff who tries to build a bridge between where he or she stands, namely in words, and the universe of images, and the bridge is made of words, but of words that advance into the meaninglessness of an abyss. This — an artificial art critic, or an electronic intermix — will not do. They will only work where universes overlap. § Every code is imperialistic. Those who stand within believe that their code is universal — that "everything" may be said in English, or in music, or in numbers. This, in fact, is the meaning of "faith." If you stand within the code of words, you believe that the word was in the beginning, that it became flesh, that it is creative (*logos spermatikos*), that it is the dwelling of Being. And if you stand in the code of numbers, you believe, with Pythagoras and Plato, that it is numbers that are real, and that through them you may achieve wisdom. The same goes for pictures, or, as Plato would say, for "ideas." But there is this moment of translation when you come up against the limits of the universe you believe in. People like the pope, and like Ludwig Wittgenstein, stand there. And art critics do too, although some of them may not always realise it. § We were told in high school to translate both as faithfully as possible and as freely as necessary. This is a curious recipe for pontification, because it opposes faith to freedom, links freedom to necessity, and says that faith is better than freedom. The recipe goes this way: if I am faithful to German, I shall translate *es gibt* by "it gives," but I will find that in this case faith does me no good. I am therefore forced into freedom, into the meaningless abyss between German and English. If I want to translate, I must give up faith and dare freedom. This is the business of bridge building in general, and especially of art criticism. Because it is not the word that is sacred, but the silent abyss that separates words from other codes and from each other. It is this sacred, meaningless, absurd abyss to which pontiffs and art critics attempt to give meaning. Now that artificial intelligences seem to do precisely that, but cannot, pontiffs are needed more than ever. *

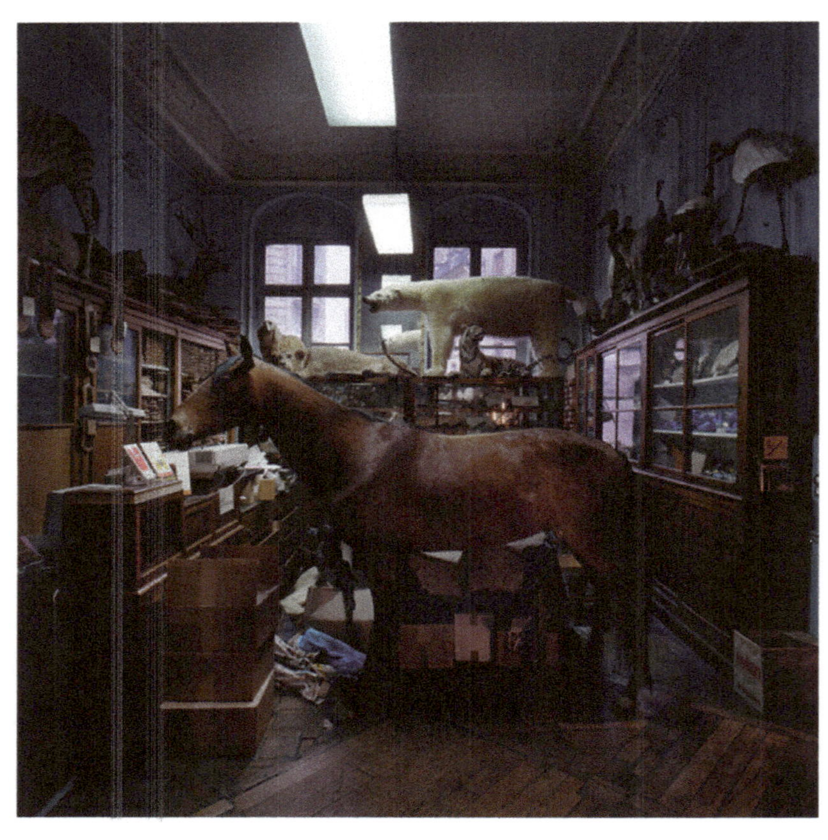

Deyrolle Taxidermy, Paris, France, 1986
Richard Ross
Ektacolor print.

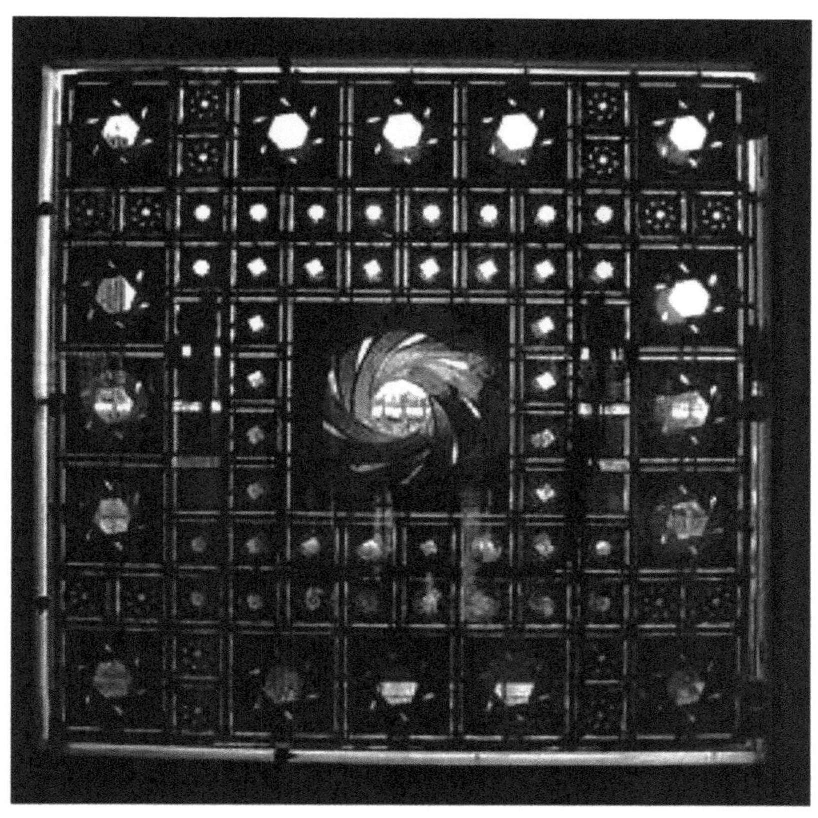

Institut du Monde Arabe, Paris, 1987
Photosensitive panels from the south façade.
Designed by Jean Nouvel, Pierre Soria, Gilbert Lézénès, and Architecture
Studio (Martin Robain, Jean-François Galmiche, Rodo Tisnado, and Jean-
François Bonne). Photo: Georges Fessy.

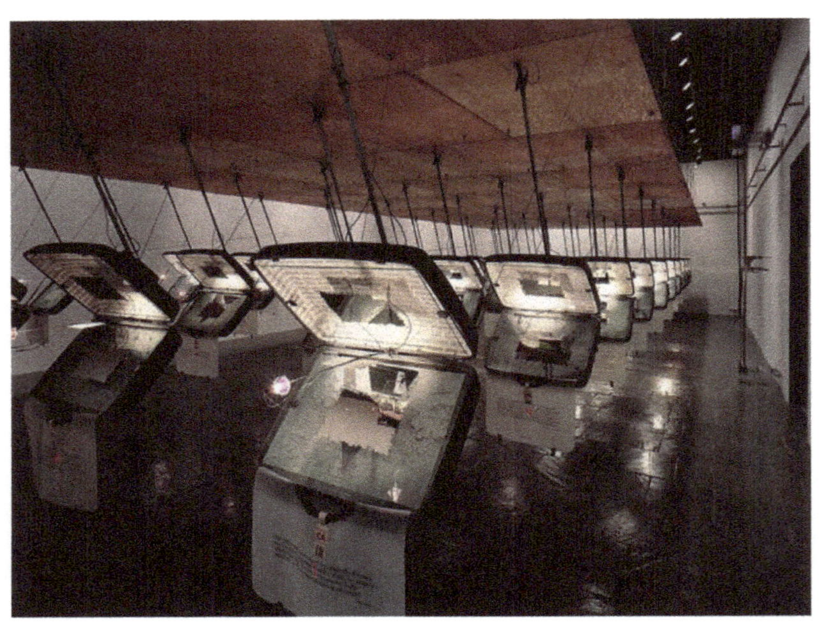

Tourisms: suitCase Studies, 1991
Elizabeth Diller and Ricardo Scofidio
Mixed media, installation view.

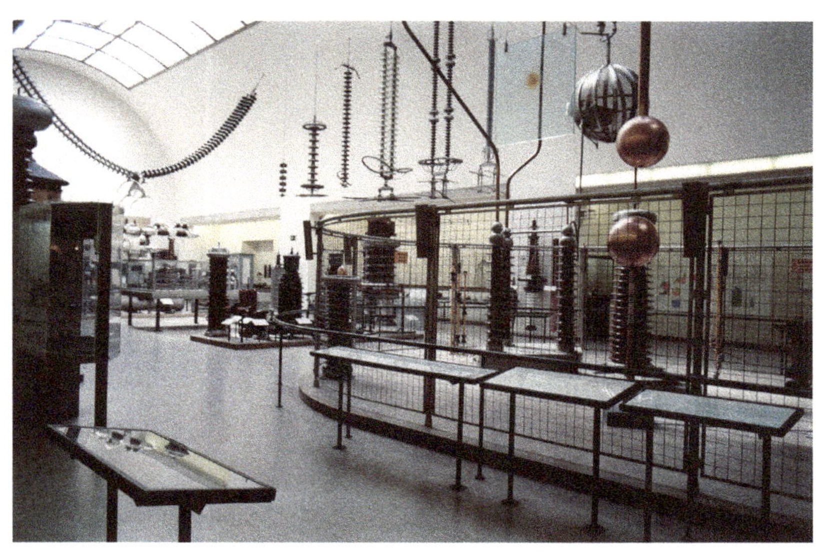

Deutsches Museum München I, 1990
Candida Höfer
Cibachrome print.

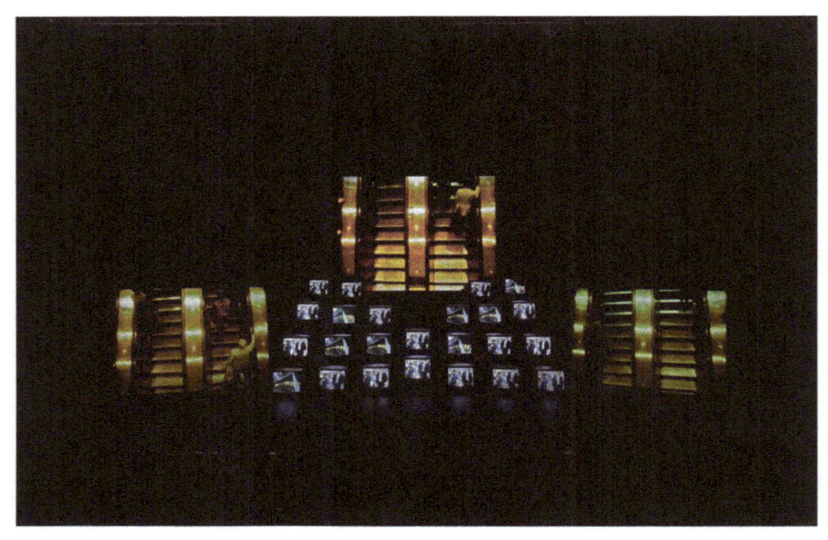

Total Recall, 1987
Gretchen Bender
Eight-channel video on 24 monitors and two rear projection screens,
approximately 18 minutes with soundtrack by Stuart Argabright.

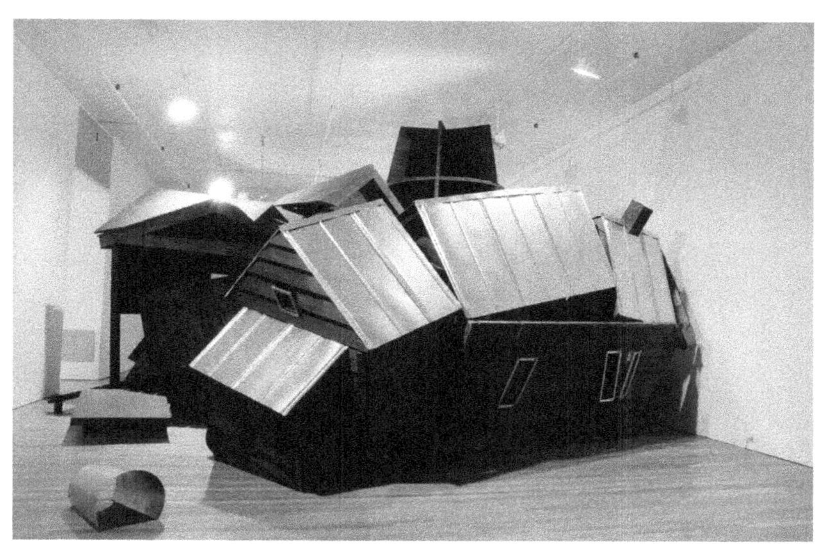

Tree Trunk with Broken Bungalow
and Shotgun Houses, 1989
James Casebere,
Installation view at Vrej Baghoomian Gallery.

ON ART AND POLITICS

Artforum
December
1990

§ Both the artist and the politician are people who do things to be exhibited in public. To Plato, in fact, "art" and "politics" were two words for the same thing. If we no longer quite share his opinion (though some of us may agree that politics is an art), it is at least partly because we no longer despise art quite as much as he did. § Plato held art and politics in contempt not because both are exhibitionists — as far as we know, he had no objection to prostitution — but because both try to impose ideas. That must involve adapting the idea to whatever it is imposed on. To Plato, the adaptation was always a betrayal. Draw a triangle, and the sum of its angles is never exactly 180°. Impose a supposedly ideal political state on people, and somehow or other it ends up not so ideal after all. To see this proven, Plato had only to look at the idea before it was imposed, and then to compare it with what the artist or politician had done to it. An artisan's table could never be as perfect as the ideal, Platonic table. To look at ideas before they were mishandled was called "theory," and revealed true ideas, and to look at them afterward was called "opinion." Plato despised both art and politics because they led to opinions, the opposite of wisdom. The lover of wisdom, the "philosopher," was the only critic of art and politics (the same thing called by different names), because he was the only one with access to true ideas.

§ Consider the procedure of the Platonic critic: a marketplace is surrounded by houses. Inside the houses are people who impose ideas on things — they take the idea of a pot, for instance, and impose it on clay, or the idea of a shoe and impose it on leather. Then they exhibit their work at their front doors. This they do because they want to exchange it for some other kind of work, the pot, say, for the shoe. The marketplace thus becomes an art forum. (Excuse the pun.) § But what criteria govern the exchange of the pot for the shoe? How does one know how many shoes the pot is worth? Enter the critic, who understands the ideas of the pot and the shoe, knows to what extent the work mishandles them, and thus knows the objects' value. So the critic (the philosopher) walks to and fro through the art forum, fixing values. He governs the marketplace — he is king of the city. (Of course his authority on pots and shoes extends also to matters political.)

§ Artists and politicians would submit to the judgment of the Platonic philosopher whether they liked it or not. They had no better criteria, and also the alternative would have been to fight it out among themselves. Take the medieval European town, ruled by the Church. Every day except Sunday it opened its gates to labourers from the surrounding fields, bringing eggs, say, and flour. They would line up the products of their economy on one side of the marketplace, opposite the pots and shoes. Then the philosopher, the bishop, would step out of his cathedral and walk through the square. The artisans and farmers must have had their own ideas about prices, but in any dispute the bishop's word was law — he was the only authorised critic, the king of the city, and if his authority was contested, there was war between town and field, and between the various neighbourhoods that housed the different trades. Thus criticism was a question of life and death, and the word of the theoretical, authorised critic was accepted "catholically," by everyone. § During the 14th and 15th centuries, however, the artisans rebelled against the philosophers, and deposed them. For the philosophers had arrived at a disagreement as to how true ideas were to be examined. One school, the realists, argued that ideas may be discovered through logic. And the other, the nominalists, thought that ideas revealed themselves only through faith (*sola fide*). If authorities quarrel, how can all their criteria be valid? The artisans and merchants took over the government of the city. Politics submitted theory to its purpose. For artisans believe not that they are betraying ideas but that they are inventing better ones, ideas that may themselves be progressively improved upon as they are imposed on different objects and people. The purpose of theory is to supply the artisans with ever better models. The result of this revolutionary submission of theory to action is modern science and technology. § Now what did this do to the philosophers, or, in their modern name,

to the intellectuals? They were expelled from government, and enclosed instead in university-like ghettos where politicians paid them to come up with new models. And the politicians divided them into two classes: one was to produce models that were useful (scientists, technicians, city planners), the other was to produce models that might amuse the politicians in their leisure hours ("artists" – philosopher-like artisans, and more useless, though more entertaining, than either). Today's intellectuals are servants and clowns. But the ghetto posed a problem: what could be done to stop the intellectuals from sneaking out of it, and back into politics? The politicians' solution was to surround the ghetto with an aura of glamour, to give intellectuals "status." The "great scientist" would become childlike in the face of the world. The "great artist" would live in splendid isolation.
§ This was not the perfect solution, however. The useful intellectuals, the scientists, kept on believing that what they were after were "true ideas," not just ways to improve industrial production. And the useless intellectuals, the artists, kept on believing

that what they were after were models for new experiences (*aisthesthai*, to experience), not just decor. This was dangerous, since the scientist might come up with models of industrial production and of government that would render the politicians useless, and the artists might prove that work was not the only source of value, and therefore that the artisan, the industrialist, was not necessarily the best person to be king of the city. The academic ghetto, in fact, created a counterrevolutionary climate, for the intellectuals never really accepted their loss of power. And the artists in the modern sense of the term — the clowns — soon opposed themselves to the artists in the classical sense (the artisans, now industrialists and politicians). This had become quite obvious by the Romantic period, when the artist and poet, children of industrialists, took to advocating industry's abolition. Some of them even preferred to die of tuberculosis in the garrets of the industrial towns than to submit wittingly to their clownship. Yet don't artists do exactly what industrialists and politicians do — impose their ideas on things? What, after all, is the ontological difference between a plastic fountain pen and a painting, or a piece of music? Aren't both the results of the imposition of ideas upon some matter — the results of a "political" opinion? § How curious. The moment that artists become kings, transforming themselves into industrialists, they create a new type of artist, their clown. But the clown denies them the right to judge him or her, submitting instead to theoretical, philosophical criticism. This sounds very funny, of course, but it is a crucial aspect of the present situation. We see another significant phenomenon if we move from the "useless" to the "useful" intellectual, for we find that work too has been divided into two different gestures, "soft" and "hard." The soft gesture explores symbols so as to spin out new models, and the hard imposes these models upon matter. The soft gesture is executed by thinkers — whom, in the end, we really must call "artists" — equipped with computers and similar apparatuses. The hard gesture, more and more, is executed not by people but by machines. § In this transformation of work, several aspects are striking. First, the actual imposition of form upon material has become mostly a mechanical rather than a human gesture. Second, people who use symbols to make models — the programmers, or the software people — are both artists (because they handle ideas) and philosophers (because they no longer apply those ideas physically). And third, there is not much sense in trying to classify intellectuals into useful and amusing ones, because the models now elaborated on computers are not only "scientific and technical" but also "artistic." § Neither Plato nor the politicians, then, have correctly anticipated the present situation. For today's intellectuals both contemplate forms, living in "theory," and handle them as well (on the computer screen). These people are artists become philosophers, or philosophers become artists. At the same time, they work without necessarily owning any machines, and without having left their ghetto. All of a sudden we have people who prove that though "theory" and "art" may fuse, "art" and "politics" may be two different ways of life altogether. § It sounded funny, a few paragraphs earlier, when I said that the artist submitted to theoretical criticism. It no longer sounds so funny, for what it means is that the artist — the programmer of work, and therefore of life — is also the theoretician. Working with computers, artists can submit their models to their own theoretical criticism before feeding them to machines that transform them into hard matter. If so, then art criticism no longer steps in after the work is done, but is part and parcel of the work's project, its program. So this is the emerging situation: artists, people who handle forms with a view to applying them, now govern the city. They are called "systems analysts," "futurologists," "technocrats," "media people," and so forth. They govern not by applying their models directly but by programming machines (and getting other people) to do the work. In this sense are they philosophers: they contemplate forms, and have a theoretical vision. Politicians may not be aware of it yet, but they have become automatons programmed by these philosopher artists. This is why we no longer agree when Plato puts art and politics in the same bag;

     politics have been deposed, and art governs the city. *

ON THREE TIMES

Artforum
February
1991

§ Once upon a time the world was a wheel: day was followed by night and night by day, winter by summer and summer by winter, birth by death and death by rebirth. About three thousand years ago that wheel changed into a stream, where everything flowed forward, nothing repeated itself, and every opportunity lost was lost forever. We know the wheel by heart and from looking at watches. We learned about the stream at school, in history class. But nowadays that stream is changing into a sand heap, the grains of which are distributed ever more evenly, though here and there they tend to fall into improbable clusters. We might have heard about the sand heap in discussions of science but we do not really grasp it yet. This is a pity, because that sand heap is a playground for art — improbable clusters of elements formed not by accident but on purpose. § When the world was a wheel, the problem was justice. The judge was time: everything had its appointed place, and people who left their place, though they were heroes, could not avoid punishment by time and in time. Time circled through the world to bring everything back to its place. The wheel world was a tragedy: one could not escape fate, which was the same thing as time, the judge and hangman. § When the world was a stream, the problem was freedom, for everything seemed to be the effect of some cause and the cause of some effect — everything was determined. But we could learn about that chain of causality with the hope of somehow manipulating it, through science and technology. (The question of how science and technology can liberate us if they are themselves determined has never been satisfactorily answered.) The stream world was a drama within which we tried to act; time flowed from the past toward the future, establishing the chain of causality. § In the world as sand heap, the problem is accident. There can be no doubt today of the general tendency toward an ever more uniform, ever more probable distribution of the particles that constitute the world. The second law of thermodynamics says so, and if we doubted that law we would have to stop believing in science, which is our only source of knowledge, and on which our daily life depends. The second law, in fact, gives us our concept of time: time is precisely the tendency toward entropy, toward a uniform distribution of the particles of matter and energy. Still, improbable, accidental clusters of particles do continue to emerge. Some are very ancient, like hydrogen and helium atoms. Others are much more recent, like the biomass on Earth, or like the human brain. § These accidents in which particles accumulate rather than disperse seem to contradict our notion of time: they are like loops in which time is reversed. One might say that these loops will return in the end to the general tendency, that they are "negatively entropic epicycles" sitting on the entropic straight line. Or one might say (as some now do) that the entropic straight line itself may prove to be a segment of a circle: that the "Thermic Death" that will eventually follow the "Big Bang" will give rise to another Big Bang, and so on forever. But neither of these solutions help, for the problem the sand heap poses is not whether time is a straight line (as it was in the stream world) or a circle (as it was in the wheel world). The problem is that time sometimes seems to run backward. If time is understood as the tendency toward an ever more probable, ever more even dispersion of particles, how can improbable situations arise (as in fact they do), and furthermore, how can such situations become even more improbable, even more complex, with time? For instance: what "negative time" was it during which hydrogen and helium atoms not only emerged themselves, but gave rise to other atom types, and those to ever more complex types of molecules, those again to the biomass, and that again to the human nervous system? § The obvious answer to this question is that the whole problem is the result of muddled thinking. Suppose we agree on the tendency toward an even distribution of particles. The sum of those particles is finite (the world is a "dosed system"); we more or less know its size (the mass of the world) and age (the age of the world). Still, the sum is very big and the world is very old. So it is not at all surprising, but to be expected, that particles should have collided accidentally with each other even while tending toward a smoother distribution. In a game of so many pieces, and of such long life, every possible accident must necessarily happen. To speak of a "negatively entropic" tendency in accidental clusters of particles such as the human brain is to have missed the whole point about the sand-heap world: accidents are inevitable in a heap this big. There is no "negative time," and no problem. § This answer might be obvious, but it begs the question. It may be a statistical inevitability that accidents will happen in the long run, but this in no way denies the fact that every individual accident is an unexpected event — a "miracle." In an overall view of the sand-heap world, the accidental emergence of the human brain seems necessary and inevitable, but if one looks at the brain as an isolated cluster of particles, the series of accidents of which it is the result seems so improbable as to force us into saying that the brain is a miracle. That cumulative series of accidents, in fact, must be seen as a "negatively entropic" process, as an "evolution." That is to say: as a process that unrolled in a time opposed to the time of the sand heap. § One thing must be retained, however, from the unsatisfactory answer to our question. Although we apparently have to admit that there are negatively entropic, evolutionary processes within the sand heap, we cannot maintain that those processes have a purpose. The results of evolution are miraculous, but evolution is still a blind and mindless game of a huge number of pointlike particles. It is true that time inverts its course in places — that the sand heap world allows for miracles. (There were no miracles in the stream world, only the effects of unknown causes.) But the sand heap world excludes a purposeful creator. It presents itself as the result not of a creative project but of blind chance. Let us look now at the three times sketched here from the point of view of what we call "values." The time of the wheel world ("magic" time) imposes moral, ethical values: crime and punishment, just retribution. It is a time for holiness, and for fear and trembling. The time of the stream world ("historical" time) imposes epistemological values: science and technology, emancipation through explanation. It is a time for disciplined action. The time of the sand-heap world ("post-Modern" time) imposes aesthetic values, and unexpected, miraculous situations. It is a time for creative artists. Magic time is ordered by the sage, historical time by the scientist, post-Modern time by the artist. § The artist is central in our time (more so than in the Renaissance) because to create is to produce unexpected, improbable situations, and we now know that the nonhuman universe does the same thing. There, however, such situations come about by chance. The artist, on the other hand, a cluster within the sand heap, turns accident into purpose. The human brain in general, in fact, is an accidental cluster that can miraculously turn accidents into purpose, a highly improbable miracle. It is the work of the artist that epitomises this process, for the artist deliberately turns time around to point to ever new information, ever less probable distributions of the grains of sand. § The three times, of course, are not completely consecutive; they overlap in our minds, our thoughts, and our feelings. We have not "overcome" circular time, which beats out the rhythm of our daily living. Historical time governs our decisions and the acts we base on those decisions. As for post-Modern, sand-heap time, it remains an uncomfortable, confusing concept, which we have not yet incorporated into our experience and thinking. Yet it is this new time that shapes artistic creation. And thus it helps to make artists more conscious of the task to which they are committed: the inversion of the absurd tendency of the world toward entropy, toward ever more probable (and therefore ever less interesting) situations. Which is to say that artists are committed against the mindless stupidity of the world. *

ON THREE SPACES

Artforum
May
1991

§ We are living tubes (worms). The world flows in through one of our openings (the mouth) to flow out again through the other opening (the anus). This is why we can distinguish between "forward" and "backward." Most of us are bilaterally symmetrical, and this is why we can distinguish between "right" and "left" (though some of us, like sea urchins, are too many-sided to do so). Originally we all trawled forward and backward, and left and right, on the beach of some Precambrian ocean, and thus there was no need or possibility for us to distinguish between "upward" and "downward." Somewhat later some of us (the birds and insects) took off from the ground, and some others (the cephalopods and humans) stood upright, though still sticking to the surface. For those who had taken off, a sphere of dimensions like "up to the right" or "down behind" opened up; for those who begun to stand upright it was instead a hemisphere that became accessible to locomotion. This may be taken to be a description of vital space, of which all other kinds of space are either derivatives or abstractions. § If you consider the hemisphere of human space you will find that it looks more like a box than a bowl, because it is shallow. We can measure the length and breadth of the space we cross in thousands of miles, but until quite recently the height of our space only measured a few yards and its depth but a few inches. This wide and long but shallow box that is our vital space is better suited for geometry (measurement of the ground) than for topology (science of space), because it consists of two dimensions to which a third has been added. We upright worms think geometrically; equations of the third degree make us nervous, and we had better leave topology to birds, bees, and angels. If we divide our vital space (*Lebensraum*), we divide it into areas, and we never fight about cubic miles (even if we have an air force). Of course we may extend that flat box of ours indefinitely by drawing a Cartesian cross, and it will then have three dimensions. Still it will not have become "real space," because it will continue to be a geometrical (not a topological) construct.

§ This flat box of ours stands still, and things move around within it. You might say that those things move with time, and that time blows through space like the wind through a room with open windows. Philosophers have thought deeply about time, and about how it relates to space, yet nobody will deny that time and space can be easily distinguished. Nobody will mistake a watch for a yardstick, unless he is crazy. Sometimes we do have a curious feeling about distances: is this place two miles away or two hours? You might also say that the distance between New York and Paris is $1,000. But these are unnecessary, idle reflections. The fact is that we live in a rigid space to be measured in miles, and that we move with a time to be measured in hours. Or at least this has been true so far.

§ But we humans have the curious ability to put ourselves in the place of somebody else: we are capable of abstraction. We can, for instance, ask ourselves how space looks from the point of view of a galaxy (of which we know, of course, that it cannot look but can only be looked at). And if we ask such a question, we find to our surprise that we cannot answer in words but only in numbers. The reason is that words are used to articulate vital space, while numbers are more abstract. (This is, by the way, a very curious reason.) Now if we articulate how space looks if seen by a galaxy, we will have to formulate equations of the fourth dimension. This is very uncomfortable, because even three dimensions like cubic miles make us nervous. But we now dispose of apparatuses that may help us to perceive such equations. They are called "plotters," and they can generate synthetic images out of numbers and show them on computer screens: we can see for ourselves what space looks like from a galaxy's point of view. We call this "outer space" or "*cosmic space*," and we even build vehicles to explore those regions closest to where we are.

§ This is not good enough, however. We may calculate cosmic space, we may imagine those calculations on screens, and we may even send machines and people there, but we cannot really understand it as long as we cannot say what it is in the words of some human language. So we must make an effort to find words to name those equations.

This, unfortunately, results in monsters like "curved space-time," an E.T.-monster (which is more horrible than anything shown in science-fiction movies) that must somehow be incorporated into common speech.

§ The result looks more or less as follows: space is just as big as it is old, namely about fifteen billion years old and fifteen billion light-years in diameter. It expands with time until time is exhausted, and this will happen when everything in space is evenly distributed. Because although space is empty, it is full of possibilities for things to happen accidentally, and for the results to be there for a time and then disappear again. The things that happen there (like the galaxies at which we look, and like ourselves) are curves within the field of the possibilities of space-time. For instance, the planet Earth is a curve within the field of gravitation of the Sun, which again is a curve within the field of the gravitation of a galaxy, which again is a curve, and so forth. You can calculate all of this in algorithms, and you can show it on a computer screen, and now that you have uttered it in so many words, you can understand it. But do you?

§ With this our capacity for abstraction is by no means exhausted. We may also abstract ourselves from our vital space and put ourselves in the place of the particles that compose us. Here the problem is different. In the case of the galaxies we may ask: what would space look like if the galaxies could look at it? But in the case of the particles we must ask: what would space look like if there were any particles we ourselves could look at? Because we may look at galaxies, but if we look for particles like quarks we see only traces. But, we might ask, if we cannot even see these particles, why should we try to put ourselves in their place? The answer is, we must do so, not only because of nuclear power and Chernobyl, but because we are able to calculate it. Now let this be put more carefully: since we cannot say exactly where a particle is, we should better say of that space not what or how it is but what and how it might be. This is why we should call it a *"virtual space,"* and only then try to understand it. § The equations that describe virtual space are even more exotic than those that calculate cosmic space, because they calculate probabilities, which is to say strictly nothing – at least nothing yet. Probability calculus states what might be, but it says even more than that. It says that reality (that which is) and unreality (that which is not) are the two horizons of probability, and that the space of particles somehow oscillates between the two. This is more or less what that monstrous term "probability wave" means. But if you try to imagine space as that sort of wave, you have not yet understood what virtual space means. You must consider two other things as well: first, anything you say about this space is more or less probable, that is, meaningless nonsense, and second, there is another monstrous term, namely, "quantic jump," and it says that a particle may jump from one orbit to another without spending time while jumping. In other words, a particle may be simultaneously at two different places within that space. Do not try to imagine such a horror (you will not succeed), but admit instead that what we are talking about is virtual time within virtual space, a not-yet-space with a not-yet-time, which is to say: we are talking about a situation in which words fail.

§ Consider what has just been said about cosmic space and about virtual space, and then consider how people all around us talk about it. Every teenager talks about cosmic space, and every artist about virtual space, as if they and everybody else knew what those words mean. One thing is certain: they mean something that does not fit into our vital space, that long and broad but flat box wherein we live for the simple reason that we are upright worms. You might say that all those people use those words because they are worms with brains attached to their mouth end. And a brain is a well-known paradox: it contains the cosmic space of which it is a part, because particles jump within the brain over nerve synapses, which means that the brain contains the virtual space that contains the cosmic space that contains the vital space in which the brain lives. But if you said so in order to explain why teenagers and artists speak about the three spaces here discussed, you would have contributed to the confusion instead of simplifying the situation. And a different sort of effort is needed if we are to understand what is happening today.

§ It is a fact that for more than a century we have been learning how to fly, and that, although we have not yet learned to do it properly, we can already experience space more or less as birds do. Another fact is that for some time now we have had things that begin with the prefix "tele-," which literally may mean "far" but which really means, "to bring nearer." Thus with the telescope we can bring things like the moon and the planets so near that they no longer look as if they are in cosmic space; thanks to the telephone we can approach people who cannot be heard and seen in vital space; thanks to the telegraph we can correspond with people over long distances as if they were in the same town in which we live; thanks to television we can see events as they happen in a quite different place within vital space; and thanks to telematics we can become neighbours with everyone equipped with the same type of apparatus. Thus that long, wide, and flat box we call our vital space is beginning to burst at its seams, and its lid is coming off to enable us to get up and leave it. § But there is another fact that may be even more decisive: we no longer have a feeling that we can trust our vital space or the time that flows through it. We are now capable of simulating things so perfectly that we can no longer distinguish them well from "true things." For instance, we can no longer say for sure whether we are watching a real or a staged scene when looking at the TV screen, or whether that voice that speaks to us is human or the voice of an apparatus. On the other hand, the fact that we can be telepresent instantly all over the place makes us doubt whether we are truly present here and now, or whether we are only dreaming. This means that we can no longer distinguish well between fact and fiction, between science and art, between the real and the unreal. Now this is a feeling that accords very well with virtual space, where true and untrue statements have literally no meaning. § If you take those two sets of facts together – on the one hand, vital space is no longer closed but is opening up to cosmic space, and on the other hand, it is becoming as untrustworthy as virtual space – you begin to understand why all those people speak about cosmic and virtual spaces. They no longer feel at home within vital space, so they are beginning to crawl out into those other spaces that can be calculated, and that everybody can contemplate on computer screens, but that nobody can understand in the true sense of that term. The upright worm that we are is beginning to take off, but nobody can say as yet where it is going, or what it is plunging into. We cannot even say whether it is going to continue to be a worm, whether it is going to be crushed, or whether it is changing into a bird or an angel. *

ON BOOKS

Artforum
November
1991

§ As material objects they are almost worthless. Their specific gravity is high, and to carry even a few of them can be an uncomfortable matter. If you move, transporting your books costs more than they are worth, and rearranging them in their new home is a nightmare. Books are a burden measurable in kilos, cubic feet, and hours. We submit to them as to an addiction: we seem in permanent need of their strings of letters, opening them up again and again to pick some of those letters out. § A Martian, in fact, or some other illiterate, might suppose that a book is a vast heap from which we gather letters one by one. The term "literature," which means "a lot of letters," would only confirm that opinion. We addicts know better: a book piles up letters only for the information encoded in their arrangement. This is its value: as information, or software. Some books contain very valuable information. And this is why we tolerate them.

§ But this is extraordinary. According to the second law of thermodynamics, nature is a system that tends to lose information. A book, then, is an unnatural object. Living beings transmit genetic information to their offspring, but not acquired information; so a book, by conveying acquired information from person to person, denies the laws of biology. In fact a book, any book, is a miracle, and we should fall on our knees every time we pick one up. § Relatively few of us actually do so, of course, though there certainly are people, even in this computer age, who attach some glimmer of reverence to the act of reading. But we also know that our books will ultimately fall into ashes just as we ourselves will, and are just as much subject to the laws of nature and of life as our bodies are. The miracle is temporary: the attempt to defy nature, to defy death, is in the long run doomed to failure in everything we do, in books as in paintings, music, architecture, science, and technology. All these energies will in time be devoured by time, by entropy, and will be forgotten. § On one level, though, books are sillier than those other efforts, for the information they store is encoded in letters. Letters are signs that represent the sounds of a spoken language. The information in a book must go through the code of language before it can be written, and to get at the information in a book you have to learn two codes: that of the language and that of the letters. This detour from thought to book by way of language is quite unnecessary, and we already have sign systems that avoid it. Numerically literate people around the world, for example, can understand each other's equations without knowing each other's languages. Furthermore, not only do letters mean sounds, but they also have to be aligned in rows, like pearls on a necklace. Books are linear and one-dimensional in structure. This is why they hold infinitely less information than two-dimensional surface structures like images, which themselves carry infinitely less information than three-dimensional structures like TV boxes. This is also why books are so heavy: being one-dimensional, they have to use vast numbers of lines to carry their information. In short, books are inefficient. § Most letter addicts probably will not accept this reasonable conclusion. The detour through language on the way from thought to book is what they love most: the information itself may even count less than the particular way in which it has been pressed into word, sequence, sonority. When we open a book we participate in a conversation that has carried and elaborated information almost since the beginning of our species. More — we become responsible for its continuation. When we look at an image our eyes scan the surface in circles, and the circle enforces eternal repetition. In a book, on the other hand, our eyes follow the lines of the text, progressively collecting the information, and thus the line carries us toward the future. Each sentence, each argument, demands the next one. The book gives us a temporal structure in which every instant is unique, and every moment lost is an opportunity lost forever. In reading a book, we experience the dramatic urgency of living. § There is something even more exciting about the linear structure of books: each row of letters points to something outside it. The line of letters "it rains" points through the English language to what you see on a grey day outside your window. But the lines also point in a quite different direction. The whole book points at its final full stop – that is what linearity is all about – but beyond that full stop the book points at its reader. Each book is a hand that reaches out for our own hand, and if we throw a book away, or even if we leave one unopened, it is as if we had amputated a hand stretched out to us.

§ The nonbookish reader pooh-poohs all this, and martials, perhaps, the following argument: before the invention of the alphabet, three and a half millennia ago, there were two types of culture. An oral (mythical) culture stored information in sound, in spoken words, and a material (magical) one stored it in hard objects. Sound, the movement of air, was fluid and malleable – to speak is almost a natural human talent – but it was fleeting, and its very fluidity opened it to noise, which deforms information. Objects like stones and bones were better storehouses of information (a Palaeolithic knife still contains the instruction "cut"), but it took a good deal of effort to imprint that information in them. And then came the alphabet, which rendered sound visible.

It unified the oral and the material, the mythical and the magical, and it overcame them both, opening the way toward historical culture. It was an incredible invention. But today we can store sound in tapes or records, and we can imprint hard objects relatively easily. We have highly efficient ways of storing and transmitting information. § Why do we need the alphabet? The fact that books continue to overflow in an inflationary wave, destroying our forests, only shows how reactionary we are, how incapable of understanding the communications revolution going on around us. § In this view, the future goes as follows: an elite of scientists and technicians uses numbers (algorithms) to articulate and communicate information. The majority is informed (and manipulated) by images — TV and advertising, say — that tend to become ever more perfect. And a few remain addicted to letters, and abhor both the numbers on one side and the images on the other. As for art, eventually the scientists' and technicians' numbers will be transcoded into images, and those numerically generated images will be constitutable as alternative virtual spaces that future artists may transform into new worlds. There will be no room for letters in such worlds, and books will disappear. § Such a vision cannot be accepted by those who love books. Will the majestic river of letters passed down to us through Homer, Dante, and Shakespeare, dividing and redividing into countless distributaries, and now reaching us in its maturity, stagnate into a muddy, swampy delta? For such lovers of literature I write this song, in praise of books, in unreasonable letters. *

ON THE TERM DESIGN

Artforum
March
1992

§ Many English words have become terms used internationally. At present this is taken to be a symptom of Anglo-Saxon predominance within the cultural realm. But the case of the term "design" is different. In its international use, "design" means something like a "pattern" or a "sketch," and the verb "to design" means something like "to make a plan for the production of some object." With this meaning the term has become important, and schools of design (industrial and otherwise) tend to become centres of cultural activity all over the world. This merits closer examination, because there are other terms (like the German "*Gestalt*" and the French "*façon*") that have similar meanings. Why was the word "design" chosen to mean an activity that is becoming ever more characteristic of our civilisation as we approach the third millennium and so-called "post-historical" existence? § In English the word "design" means (among other things) a "sinister scheme, a secret project, an aggressive intention, a plot, an evil purpose." There are other terms that have similar insidious, cunning, deceitful connotations. One of them is "machine," another is "mechanisms." The Greek *"mechos"* means a contrivance for the purpose of cheating, a machination. A typical machine is the Trojan horse, and its builder, Ulysses, is called by Homer *polymechanikos*, which means "trickster." In fact, "mechanics" should be translated as "the science of cheating." Another such term is "technical." The Greek word *"techné"* means the skill of a carpenter (*tekton*), and the idea behind it goes as follows: there is shapeless matter, mostly wood (*hylé*), and a specific skill is needed to press it into a shape (*morphé*). Philosophers, especially Plato, have discussed that idea. They have shown that shapes are distorted when applied to matter, and that, therefore, the skill to apply them (*techné*) amounts to devious treason: technicians are people who seduce people to admire contemptible matter like stone by shaping it into statues. In fact, "MIT" could be said to mean "Massachusetts Institute for the Teaching of Skilful Swindlers." The Latin translation of *techné* is *ars*, the skill of joining things together. The diminutive of *ars* is *articulum* (little art), which means knuckle. Thus "to articulate," means to twist one's little finger skilfully, and an "article" (like the one you are reading) means a skilful little twist to deceive you. You can feel that meaning in terms like "artful," "artifice," and "artificial." Thus an artist is one who is more or less good at cheating. § Now consider the terms "design," "machine," "technical," and "art" together. They mean, all of them: methods for cheating, various forms of cunning. But each of those terms has a different meaning on the surface of cultural discourse. So different, are those surface meanings, that ever since the end of the Renaissance the deeper meaning that connects them to each other has been suppressed and, therefore, has tended to be forgotten. Modern, bourgeois civilisation has divided culture into two sharply opposed branches: the "hard" one, with its machines and technicians, and the "soft" one with its artists. This fateful divorce between the mechanic and the artist became impossible to maintain at the close of the 19th century, when it became ever more obvious that the one cannot live without the other. At that point, the term "design" stepped in to bridge the gulf between the two cultures. § Those who still adhere to the surface meanings of the terms "machine" and "art" will probably say that "design" means that area where mechanical and artistic skills and activities overlap, and that, therefore, the growing importance of design shows how the two modern cultures are merging. But those who think that the meanings of "machine" and "art" are fundamentally identical will have a different view of our situation. They will tend to see that the increasing importance of design (and of schools of design) is a proof of our increasing awareness of what we are doing when we commit ourselves to culture. Such persons will argue that all four terms – "design," "machine," "technical," and "art" – mean cheating, that these are the central cultural terms, and that the use of the term "design" shows that we are beginning to understand that we cheat consciously when we commit ourselves to cultural activities and endeavours. § Let this be illustrated. A lever is a simple machine (although it does not look like one) designed to simulate a human arm. Its technique is very old, probably older than our species. Thus "machine," "design," "art," and "technique" cannot be thought apart from one another where the lever is concerned. Now the purpose behind the lever, its intent, is to cheat gravitation so that heavy bodies may be lifted in spite of their heaviness. The lever is a machine designed technically to cheat nature. The object of art (the artificial arm) is more powerful than nature and its laws. § Archimedes saw that if you find a point of support for your lever, you may lift the whole world off its hinges. The lever is a machine designed to transcend nature, and if we use it artfully, we may become gods and fall back on nature from above like a *deus ex machina,* and thus govern the laws of nature. § This example may be extended to the entire realm of culture. Culture as a whole is a design to cheat nature, to outwit it, and everything in it is designed to deliver us artificially from our mammal condition, to make free artists of us all. But now consider what is implied in such a late glorification of plotting, of scheming, of insidious cunning. Take a plastic fountain pen as an example. Plastic fountain pens are becoming ever cheaper, so much so that they are often distributed free of charge, tending toward becoming worthless. (Note that "worthless" does not mean "useless.") The material plastic fountain pens are made of is even more shapeless than wood (*hylé*), and we need no Platonic philosophers to show that it is worthless (nothing to be admired). Modern analysts, and especially Marxists, have shown that the value of an object lies not in the material of which it is made but in the labour that produced it. In the case of the plastic fountain pen that work was done by technically highly developed machines, which has cheapened the product to a point where it is worth nothing. The entire value of the plastic fountain pen is in its design (which enables it to write), and in the design of the machine that produces it. § If you now consider the design of the fountain pen and of the machine that produces it, you will find that they represent a conjunction of several very complex ideas from pure science, applied science, aesthetics, economy, social psychology, and even disciplines like mathematics. This coming together of complex ideas is highly creative: the design of the plastic fountain pen shows an accumulation of intelligence, imagination, and intuition. Still, fountain pens tend to be distributed free of charge, which means that they are thrown away after having been used, that they are contemptible gadgets.

§ This example (like the one of the lever) may be extended to the whole of culture. We are becoming ever more conscious of the fact that culture is a design against our natural condition, that each and every artefact is intended to cheat nature around us and within us, and that the term "design" means the very essence of culture. This awareness implies that we are designing ever better. Mechanics, techniques, and the arts have begun to melt and to constitute one single commitment. Everything is thus becoming ever more functional, ever more beautiful, ever more powerful. And for the same reason it is becoming ever cheaper. The whole of culture is becoming ever more a set of contemptible gadgets. § It now appears that a possible answer to the question of why we use the word "design" is precisely because it implies a sinister scheme, an evil purpose. As that activity named "design" becomes ever more characteristic of our situation, it becomes ever more evident that the whole of civilisation is a cunning device to cheat us. As we approach the third millennium, we begin to learn to outwit culture, to scheme against the schemes that are designed to cheat us. We now know that nothing about culture is real: everything is a cunning attempt at cheating, at substituting the fake for the real. Our hospitals may be designed like deluxe hotels, and our deathbeds may be designed like works of art, but we must all die like mammals. The more we become aware of what "design" means, the more we lose faith in mechanics, in technology, in the arts, and the less we trust culture. § This new mistrust in fakes, this incapacity to accept them at face value, this loss of the sense of value, may be what the term "post-history" means, namely a period in which "design" will reacquire all the connotations it had lost during history, a time in which we are forced to face nature within us and without us. "Posthistory" may be that terrible period when designs no longer work, because, finally, we have learned too much about them. *

† Artforum Editor's note: It was with great sadness that the editors of Artforum heard recently of the death of Vilém Flusser, a distinguished writer and teacher of communications and a regular contributor to these pages. A number of Professor Flusser's columns for Artforum, completed but unpublished at the time of his death, will appear in the magazine in future issues.

ON PROGRESS

Artforum
Summer
1992

§ Both of our eyes look ahead (unless we turn our heads), and both of our feet point in the same direction (unless we make a dance step). This is why the idea that our way of life follows a straight line seems to be reasonable. But if we examine the matter more closely, we find that progressive ideologies are mistaken. If we imagine that we walk on a surface on which our steps could leave traces, we shall discover a pattern similar to the one that underlies the traffic in an anthill. Our ways of life (be they American or otherwise) are not straight lines that lead from birth to death; instead they are composed of crossings and recrossings. For those of us who lead settled lives, most of our steps lead in and out of doors, and this is why they crisscross. It therefore looks like we need to abolish doors to be really progressive. But this might have undesirable consequences. § When we step outdoors, we do so to enter the world. But we run the risk of losing ourselves there. So we step back indoors to find ourselves again, and thus run the risk of losing the world. Stepping in-

and outdoors is a risky business, but it is in taking this risk that we become conscious of ourselves and the world. The door is a tool for acquiring consciousness, because it establishes a distinction between the private and the public and links both regions. If there were no doors, we would be unable to publish and privatize, and there would be no home or Republic. This is why we are not disposed to sacrifice doors for progress.

§ Suppose that you have accepted the argument that sedentary people cannot be progressive. You might now expect nomads like hunters, shepherds, or visiting professors, to follow the straight line. They seem to live in open spaces, they are public figures, and thus free to follow the tips of their noses. However, you will find that this is not so. On their way toward death they do not follow their, noses but some purpose like deer, sheep, or academic honors. This leads them astray, and their ways of life become distorted. Nomads are just as incapable of real progress as settlers, and erratic confusion seems to be the lot of us humans. Unless, of course, the term "progress" is given a different meaning.

§ There can be no doubt that to live means to walk toward death, because it is a fact that to live is to move, and because outside of death there is no other direction. Those who stay in bed and never get up, try to deny this, but by doing so they prove why the rest of us get up in the morning. If we did not expect to die there would be no hurry, and we could stay in bed forever. Now, on our way toward death, we come up against one obstacle after another. The Latin word for obstacle is *"ob-iectum"* and the Greek one is *"problema."* On our way, we bump up against one object after another, and these objects are problems. We overcome objects, we solve problems, one by one, and the sum total of this may be called "progress". § If by "progress" we mean accumulated problem solving, we are committed to a curious position. For instance: the American way of life is more progressive than that of Australian aborigines, because Americans have solved more problems. The question here is: who counted the problems, an American, an Australian aborigine, or some third party? Can it be that progress is a term relative to an accountant? What about the various political parties all over the world who call themselves "progressive?" Can it be that each of these parties offers a different account of the problems it claims to have solved, and the problems it considers worthy of solving? Which reminds one of Darwin. Each and every species now in existence is the most progressive of them all, because it solved all the problems that stood in its way, which is why it has not (yet) been extinguished. From its own point of view, the AIDS virus is more progressive than the human species because it has survived all attempts to eliminate it; it has solved all its problems. This is not a very satisfactory definition of "progress." § Mozart's *Don Giovanni* offers a way out of this dilemma. Leporello recites a list of the women Don Juan has conquered so far, revealing that their number is a thousand and three in Spain alone, not including all the other countries. This implies a different definition of "progress." There is a purpose. In Don Juan's case: the conquest of all the women in the world. But any other purpose is just as defensible as a definition of "progress," be it money, fame, the establishment of Heaven on Earth, or the Islamic *Ummah*. One thousand and three women in Spain are the measure of Don Juan's progress toward his purpose. He is a cultural hero in Western civilization, because he is so extraordinarily progressive. He is progressive because he has broken the record of a thousand women. The American way of life, like Don Juan's, is extraordinarily progressive, having broken so many records - no matter what the purpose. This, by the way, is the principle computers stand on. A purpose is fed to them and they approach it with record-breaking speed by progressive additions. Don Juan is a mythical computer: out of 1,003 sexemes (or sexels), he approaches progressively total sex computation. Thus Mozart's opera shows what "progress" has come to mean, and where it leads. § Let us reconsider Don Juan's problem. He aims at conquering all the women in the world. Logic tells us that instead of saying "all women,", we may say the class *Woman*. Don Juan aims at conquering *the* woman. And his strategy is called "induction." He tries to get at *Woman*, in a general sense, by adding one special woman after another, until the whole class is exhausted. This is not a very intelligent strategy, and "progress" in this sense, is not a very intelligent way of living. There is a better way to get there. *Woman* in general is contained in each and every special woman. This is why each woman is a member of the class *Woman*. He who has conquered this "*Woman*-ness," which is hidden in every woman, has achieved more, than if he had conquered all the women in the world. And this proposes yet another meaning of the term "progress." § This may be put as follows: each and every object (problem) that I encounter on my way contains a nucleus; a central point which, somehow, connects it to all the problems in the world. If I could really solve a single problem, I would have solved all the mysteries in the world. The reason I cannot do so, why I cannot really solve even one problem, is doubly complex. Each object in the world is surrounded by an infinite number of points of view, and it can be exhausted (solved) only if all those infinite points of view are applied to it. The moment I assume one of these infinite points of view, however, the problem reveals itself as my own projection, and it involves me. § To give an example, let a drinking glass be my problem. It is surrounded by an infinite number of points of view, for instance the point of view of chemistry, of the glass markets, of the history of Western art, and of industrial production. I cannot assume them all, because I shall die long before I even begin to jump from one to the other. But I know that if I could assume them all, I could solve all the problems in the world. So I take at least one point of view, and I look at the drinking glass from my present position. It appears to have a circular shape, but, of course, I know this is only my own projection. If I had looked sideways at the glass, its shape would have been elliptical, or a straight line. I am involved in the problem of the drinking glass the moment I have assumed a point of view with regard to it, and if I change my point of view, I change just as much as the drinking glass.

§ This simple example was offered to show where Don Juan was mistaken. He believed that it was possible to add one woman to another to get at *Woman*, and that this could be done without involving himself in the process. The result was that the Man of Stone ("*uomo di sasso*") took hold of him. It was the lack of involvement that was Don Juan's undoing. If I want to solve the problem of the drinking glass, I get involved in it, it swallows me up, I forget myself in it, and the nearer I get to the centre of the problem, the more I lose myself within it. This is the true reason why I cannot really solve even a single problem: I am no longer really there, long before I approach the centre. This is as true of the drinking glass as it is with each and every problem, but with *Woman* it is not only true, but mysteriously sacred. § On my way, I encounter a woman, and in this sense, she is like the drinking glass: an object, a problem. But as I approach her in my desire for her, she herself approaches me, because I am, myself, her problem. This mutual encounter reveals the infinity of points of view, which surrounds both of us, and which may be called "recognition of each other." A lifetime is far too short to even begin to exhaust that recognition. And the traditional name for this life-long attempt at mutual recognition is "love" (although that word may have become suspect). Of course, this does not solve any problem. Each one is lost within the other long before the solution is reached, and thus has forgotten what he (and she) were after. Don Juan's method of computing sexels is stupid, because it is incapable of being self-effacing, which is the only way to approach any solution.

§ The purpose of this reflection on progress was to suggest that there is a meaning to this term which may help us to understand why we do whatever we do. To progress may not mean to advance, to go from one thing to another. Instead, it may mean to return over and over to a very few points, in an effort to get involved with them, and thus go into them ever deeper. Of course, this meaning of progress has always been the sign that distinguishes greatness. Mozart comes back over and over again to the same problem of harmony, Van Gogh to the same problem of colour, Newton to the same problem of force over distances, Plato to the same problem of form. As they come back to it, over and over again, they progress. But the important thing about this is the self-forgetting that marks that progress: this "love," this "fidelity," this opening oneself up and letting oneself be swallowed.

§ We have computers at our disposal. These Don Juan machines show what progress means if we understand it as step-by-step problem solving. But we also have photo cameras, which are tools for assuming points of view as they surround objects. A photo camera progresses not by advancing from object to object (if it does so it has betrayed the principle it stands on). A camera progresses if it reveals ever-new aspects of one single object. A camera is a tool for a "phenomenological vision." This whole reflection was intended to show that progress may have a phenomenological meaning. We should take photo cameras and not computers as models for progress. If we do so, we might avoid not death, of course, but the man of stone who is waiting for us, and whom so many prophets of doom are predicting as the wages of progress. *

† *This essay has been re-edited from Flusser's original typescript. The version published in 1992 after his death had been considerably shortened so it was decided that for this edition the essay should be restored to its original length.*

FOR ARTFORUM

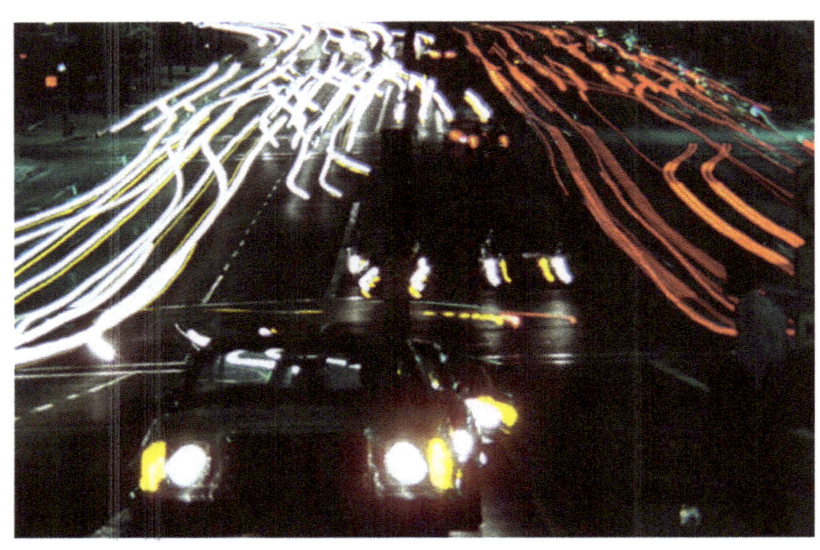

Koyaanisqatsi, 1983
Godfrey Reggio
Still from color film (Photo: Phototeque).

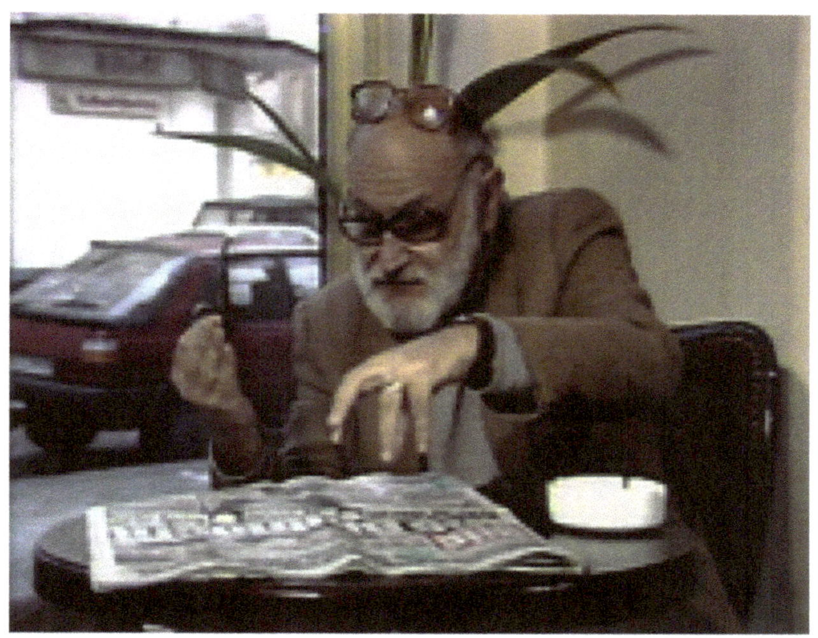

Catchphrases-Catchimages:
A Conversation with Vilém Flusser, 1986
Harun Farocki
Still from the 13 minute video in which Flusser and Farocki discuss the
arrangement of text and images on the front page of the daily tabloid
newspaper *Bild Zeitung*.

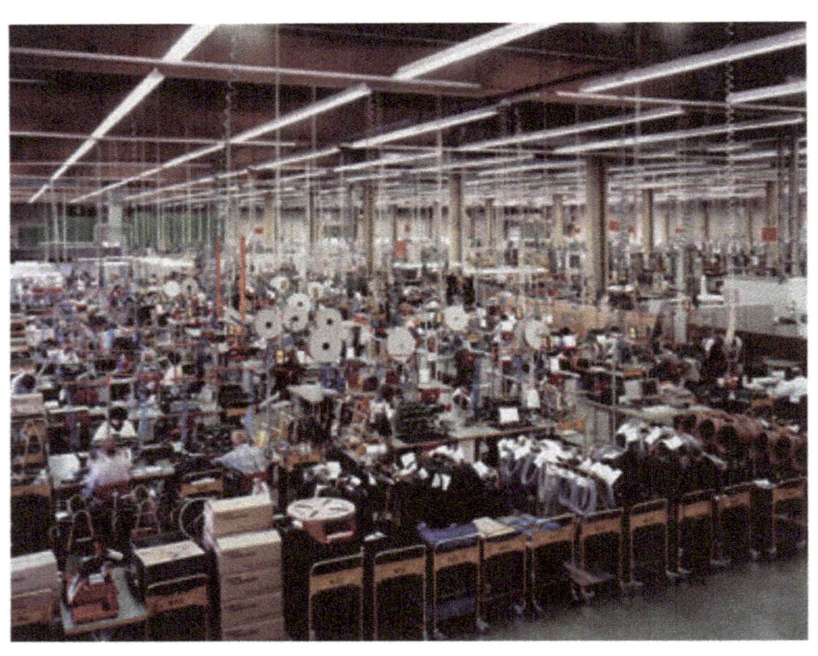

Karlsruhe, Siemens, 1991
Andreas Gursky
Color photograph © Andreas Gursky 1991. Artists Rights Society (ARS),
New York, VG Bild-Kunst, Bonn. Courtesy Sprüth Magers, Berlin-London.

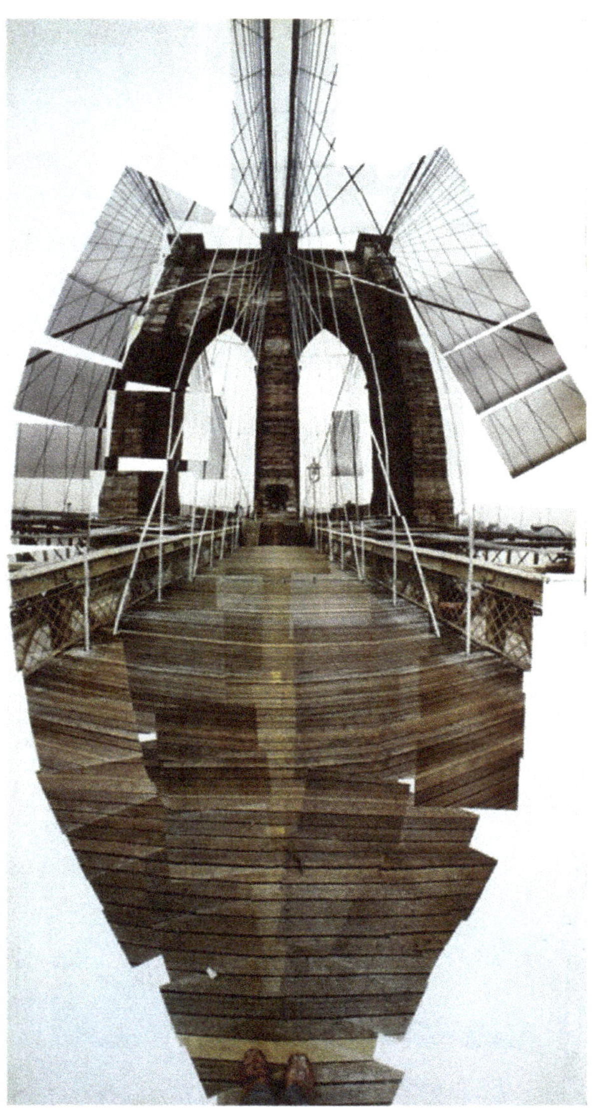

The Brooklyn Bridge, Nov. 28th, 1982
David Hockney
Photographic collage.

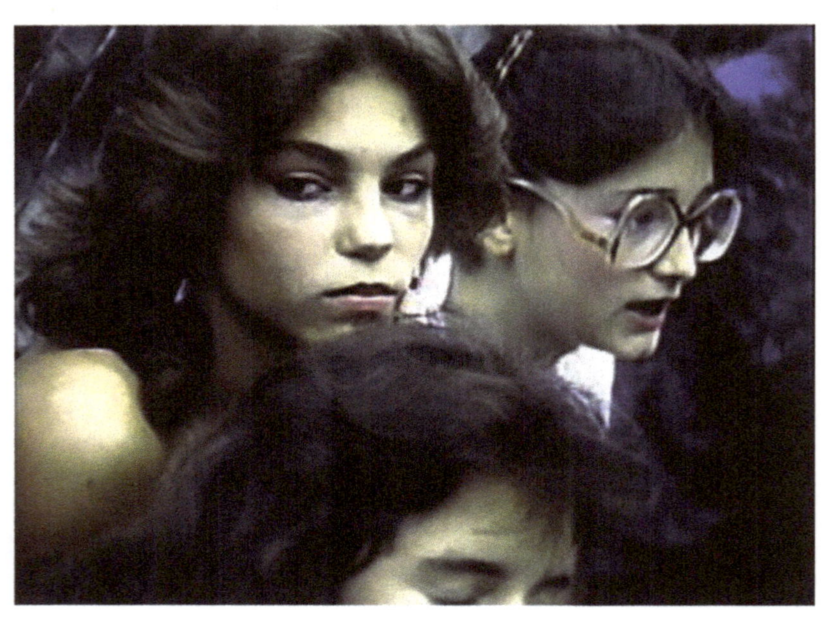

Evocation of Faust: Charming Landscape, 1987
Dara Birnbaum
Video still from the trilogy *Damnation of Faust*.

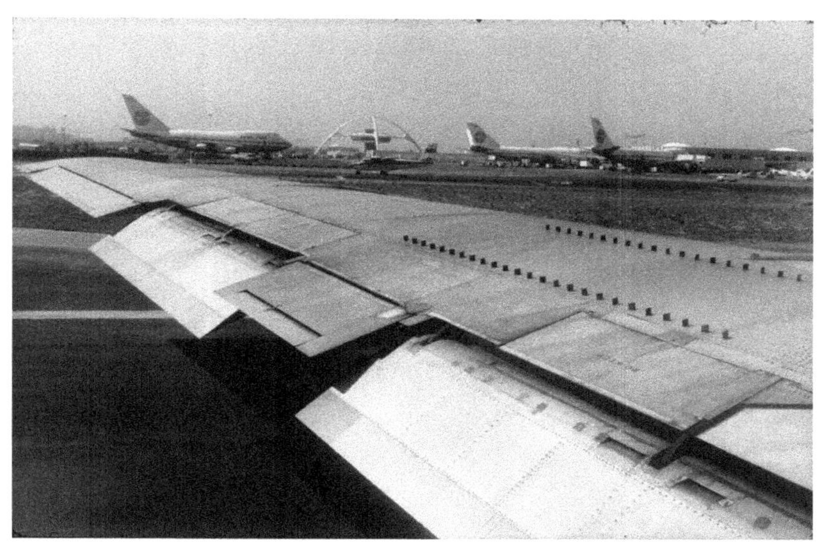

Los Angeles Airport, 1978-83
Garry Winogrand
Gelatin silver print, printed by Tom Consilvio in 1987, 8 3/4 x 13 1/16"
© The Estate of Garry Winogrand, courtesy Fraenkel Gallery.

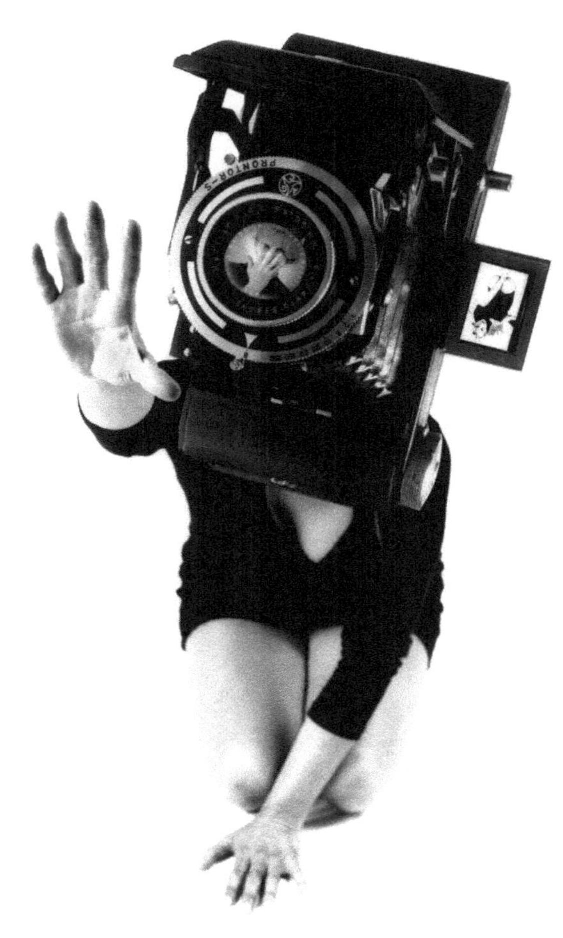

Reach (Phantom Limb Series), 1986
Lynn Hershman Leeson
Silver gelatin print. Courtesy Bridget Donahue; Anglim Gilbert.

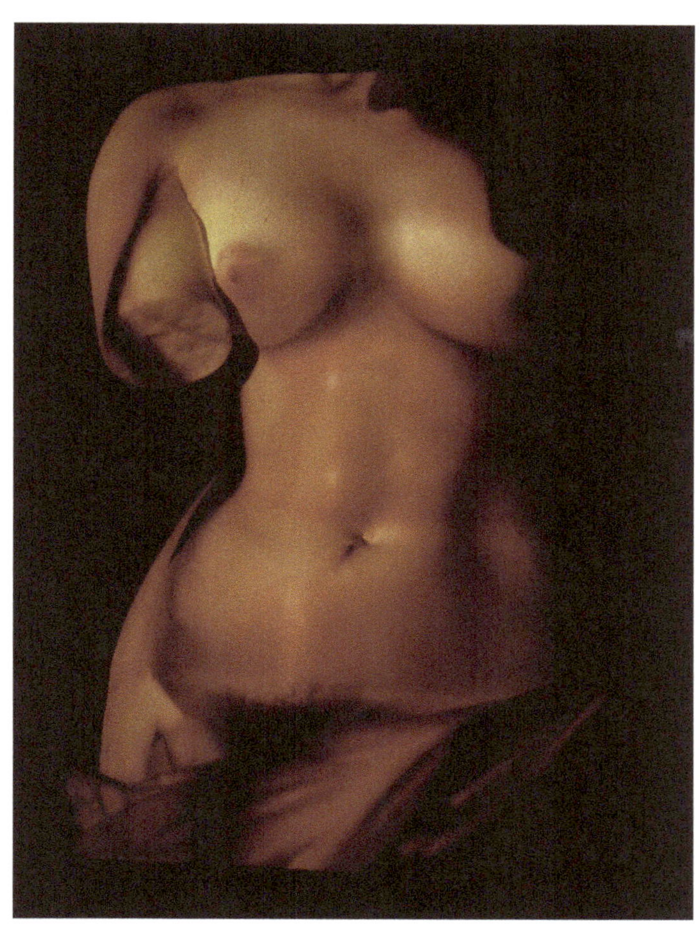

Untitled (Meeting With Venus de Milo Series), 1991
Lizzie Calligas
Cibachrome.

ON SANDWICHES,
A POSTMODERN REFLECTION

Originally
unpublished

§ "Chaos is undiscovered order, and order is undiscovered chaos." The first part of this statement is an article of modern faith: every apparently chaotic phenomenon obscures order and it is the business of reason to pierce this illusion and discover that order. The second part of the statement is an articulation of modern despair: everything which appears to be orderly floats upon an absurd mass of chaos into which we were thrown at birth without being consulted. The two parts of this statement seem to contradict each other and the modern age oscillates between the poles of this contradiction. On the one hand, faith in the progress of reason (pure and applied science); on the other, the deep-rooted existential conviction that every human effort is in vain in the face of death. We know of the barbarous atrocities which have marked the two extremes of that oscillation during the last stages of the modern age: the murderous attempts by "leftist" totalitarian regimes to force the unruly behaviour of individuals and societies into what they hold to be an underlying order; and of the even more murderous appeal to irrational behaviour by "rightist" totalitarianisms.

§ But the two parts of this statement do not in fact contradict each other. What the statement means is this: if reason penetrates disorderly phenomena far enough, it will discover some order, and if it penetrates this order even further, it will discover disorder. This statement implies that both the objective and the subjective world have a sandwich structure: they are composed of alternating levels of order and disorder. An example of the objective sandwich is the disorderly motion of snowflakes, which hides orderly motion (for instance free fall) – and that orderly motion hides a disorderly one (for instance, particle jumps in physics). An example of the subjective sandwich is when an orderly (rational) act hides disorderly psychic motives and that disorder obscures some orderly psychic system. In fact, the statement suggests that each and every phenomenon – physical, biological, psychic, or social – will under analysis reveal a sandwich structure. Gödel's theorem shows that even highly ordered systems such as logic and mathematics have this structure.

§ How are we to visualise this sandwich and live with it? Is it like a building comprised of an infinite number of stories, wherein the elevator of reason ascends and descends from victory to defeat and from defeat to victory? Or is it more like a loop composed of successive layers, wherein the "last" level precedes the "first" somewhere outside our field of vision? Are we to trust reason, because it accumulates victory after victory, or are we to give up hope in reason, because it goes from defeat to defeat? § Let us have a closer look at the sandwich. At first glance, its levels do not seem to be neatly separated. Each level is a fuzzy set that invades the fuzzy sets above it and below it. Grey zones stand between the levels. For instance, nuclear phenomena seem to occur in a grey zone between orderly orbits and the disordered jump of particles. Upon second glance, however, the fuzziness is not within the sandwich but within the phenomenon it analyses. It is the phenomenon that is grey.

§ For example: a cat chases a mouse. This phenomenon ranges within the sandwich level "animal behaviour," which is a disorderly one; and within the sandwich level "niches within an ecosystem," which is an orderly one; and within the sandwich level "origin of species by chance mutations," which is one of disorder. How does the cat chase? In a chaotic fashion? Or according to the order imposed on it by its ecosystem? Or in a fashion imposed on it by its genetic information, which is a chance product? These are, of course, not the right questions. The cat chases as it will; it does not chase within the sandwich. It is the sandwich that separates the chase into meat levels of order and disorder. The sandwich is black/white/black (order following disorder, followed by disorder); the cat's chase is grey; and the whole purpose of the sandwich is to analyse that greyness.

§ However, although the sandwich is neither fuzzy nor grey, it is a curious sandwich. Each level contains phenomena shared by other levels. Does this mean the levels contain each other like Russian dolls? Undoubtedly, the sandwich is more like a set of Russian doll than a steadfast rule: the "ecosystem" layer is contained within the "animal behaviour" layer. But it is also like a reversible Russian doll system: the "animal behaviour" layer is contained within the "ecosystem" layer. Is a small doll able to hold a large one, like the human brain, which holds the universe that contains it? The sandwich is contorted into a kind of Russian doll cannibalism, each layer attempting to devour the others. It is contorted, because it tries to distinguish order from disorder in the grey concreteness of the world around and within us.

§ The sandwich invites us to accept the greyness of the concrete world as a point of departure — or, to put it more dynamically, to accept the fact that everywhere around and within us order emerges from disorder and recedes back into disorder. Considered in isolation, this is a very banal statement. But within the Sandwich context it is anything but banal because it invites us to abandon some of modern civilisation's basic beliefs and values and challenges us to create a new civilisation. § If we accept the sandwich (as we must, given the present stage of scientific knowledge), we have to accept that the search for fundamental order is in vain — not for practical but theoretical reasons, because a fundamental order containing all the other levels must rest on a disorderly level that contains all the other levels along with it. This implies that we have given up modern science, a discipline in search of that fundamental order — a "*mathesis universalis*" or "universal combinatory game of theorems and algorithms." If we admit (as we must), that science can never (for theoretical reasons) achieve fundamental knowledge, and therefore can never provide us with mastery over the world and ourselves, then modern science is over. § However, there is no doubt that we owe the existence of the sandwich itself to modern science. The sandwich shows us that scientific method is not limited in its competence to orderly levels and that it must capitulate when it reaches disorderly levels. Instead, it shows us the exact opposite: the scientific method is competent to penetrate any disorderly level and discover some order beneath it. It is precisely because science stumbles over and over again, because it bangs itself repeatedly against disorderly levels, that it can penetrate ever deeper into the concrete greyness of the phenomenal World. Thus the sandwich forces us to admit that science is incompetent on some fundamental level, but competent enough to advance indefinitely. § It boils down to this: we have to redefine science and its place within the fabric of civilisation. We can no longer conceive of science as a search for "truth" (unless we redefine that word). Instead, we have to conceive of it as a method for carving various levels of order out of the concrete greyness surrounding us and within us — like a sculptor who carves a figure from the greyness of marble. Was that figure within the marble before the sculptor began to carve it? Were those orders within the phenomena before science delineated them? These are typically postmodern questions. In other words: we have to redefine science as one amongst the art forms, and we have to define the sandwich (the scientific model), as a sort of chisel. This will have profound consequences for postmodern civilisation. § Modern civilisation is divided into two unequal branches that have great difficulty communicating with one another: scientific and technical culture and artistic culture. This division is due to the modern belief that science "discovers" while the arts merely "invent." This is precisely what we no longer believe: that scientific reason adequately explains, with mysterious "harmony," the fundamental structure of the world. The sandwich would have us accept that all the orders science "discovers" were previously invented within the sandwich and the "laws of nature" that science discovers were injected previously into nature by the sandwich. This is precisely what the sculptor and all the arts do. Scientific method differs from all other artistic methods, just as all other methods differ from one another. But the scientific method is an extraordinarily powerful one. Hence, postmodern civilisation can no longer maintain the division between science and the arts and will reestablish a unity lost during the Renaissance. § This is easier said than done, however, because the fusion of science and art poses some formidable problems. If we admit that science is an art form (and therefore that the arts are all branches of science), we abandon the distinction between discovery and invention, between "truth" and "fiction." The sandwich under consideration becomes as true and/or fictitious as a poem, a painting, or a musical composition. It becomes as much a work of art as each of these — which implies a definition of "truth" we are far from achieving. But what we can say, even now, is that the sandwich (this scientific model), is a glorious work of art: a kind of immaterial cathedral erected by scientific reason. This is a postmodern way of understanding it.

§ This is only one view among many, however. Previously unimagined and inconceivable perspectives open up when we learn to substitute faith in modern science (which now appears naïve) with a more sophisticated attitude. If we accept that science is an art form and that the arts are epistemological disciplines, we allow for science and all other arts to develop in close communication with each other. The results of this fusion are too staggering to envision at the present stage of civilisation. But the current decay of faith in science (noticeable everywhere — and most particularly within scientific texts) need not have pernicious effects. Modern civilisation will not necessarily be followed by technocratic barbarism (the uncritical application of science) or irrational bestiality (the abandoning of science and reason). It may be followed by a postmodern civilisation in which reason is liberated from unreasonable expectations and allowed to develop more fully. This is the meaning of the sentence with which this paper begins. *

ABOUT LEVERS

Originally
unpublished

§ He who finds a point of support may lift the world from its hinges. This is the principle of the lever, and the man who discovered it was not Archimedes. It must have been his predecessor in the Neander Valley, unless the lever is an even more ancient invention. This article will try to consider some aspects of that invention, because the writer suspects that the whole process called "human history" (more aptly, "the anthropoid process of humanisation") is linked closely to levers. A word of caution, however: although the lever is a machine meant to lift objects, this article will not necessarily be uplifting. § The lever is a machine, which means that it is a trick intended to cheat something. The lever is a machine that cheats heavy bodies out of their heaviness, and it does so without taking them lightly. In this, the lever behaves like some Oriental fighters: it uses the strength of its adversaries to defeat them. Mechanics may be the Western form of Judo: it combats nature by turning its laws against itself. Here on Earth (where we all live provisionally), the bodies are all heavy. They tend toward the centre of our planet. Levers were invented to do something about this terrestrial tendency downward. Heavenly bodies appear to be different. They appear to be circling weightlessly, forever. But Newton has shown that heavenly bodies are just as down-to-Earth as all other bodies: he unified terrestrial and celestial mechanics. He showed, for instance, that some day in the distant future the planet Mercury will fall accidentally into the Sun, just as the famous apple fell accidentally (necessarily) upon his own head. By doing so, Newton lifted the Earth and all bodies on it (including our own) into Heaven. No need to commit oneself to the establishment of Heaven on Earth: Newton already did so. Unfortunately, however, Heaven is just as down-to-Earth as our bodies. The lever is just as competent here on Earth as it is in Heaven. § All bodies are heavy, and if they are up, sooner or later they will come down. We ourselves are heavy bodies, and according to our tradition we have already fallen. Plato thought we had fallen from the realm of eternal ideas into the realm of mere appearances, and Judæo-Christians believe we have fallen from Paradise into this sorry world. Even if this were so, however, and we are fallen men and women, some of us try to rise and stand upright. We even call an early ancestor *"Homo erectus,"* the Upright Man, to show that we have not been knocked out by Platonic oblivion or Judæo-Christian sin, that we are still fighting. Which lever did we use to stand upright? How did we cheat the heaviness of our bodies? Let us look mechanistically at that question. Let us suppose that we have not fallen from Platonic ideals or Paradise, but two million years ago from East African tree tops. Try to imagine the situation: there is a forest and in the trees live heavy-bodied animals like chimpanzees and gorillas. Although they fall like other heavy bodies, they stay up because they have developed a few acrobatic tricks in the course of evolution. They have survived because they are fit for the Darwinian circus. And then, per Nietzsche, each day grows colder, the trees become fewer, and the distance between them wider. Suddenly these anthropoid acrobats are no longer fit for survival. No complex probability calculus is needed to understand that, as they jump from treetop to treetop, accidents become more frequent. These accidents, which become more inevitable in the new traffic situation, should end the anthropoid story. Instead, these inevitable accidents constitute the Origin of Man (and no doubt Woman, too), because not all of the fallen anthropoids break their backs when they fall upon the savannah, which has now taken the place of the forest. Some of them survive, although they are savannah misfits — and we are their descendants. § Before considering how these misfits became *Homines erecti,* one thing must be kept in mind: there were very few survivors. The ecological catastrophe that swept through East Africa two million years ago wiped out most of the treetop dwellers. If one tries to intuit such a scenario, one can see how the heavy bodies of a few hairy apes fell heavily upon the ground and struggled, somehow, to get up. Such a heavy fall must have caused a great impression on the inhabitants of the savannah; the whole ecosystem must have trembled. Maybe we can hear the impact of that fall even now, in the lamentations of the eco-fanatics, just as we hear the echo of the Big Bang, as background noise in the Cosmos. It is difficult to imagine that there were few potential humans around at the time and that each one of them was important. Now there are between five and six billion survivors of that catastrophe and, since they are all statistically equal, each one is just as important as the others — which is to say, unimportant. They assemble in the hundreds of thousands, in open spaces, lifting their arms with open palms or closed fists toward the sky and shouting, and every horse with a policeman on its back is more prominent than the humans in the crowd. Two million years ago, every potential human being was prominent, and it is in this anti-statistical, anti-democratic climate that the lever must have been invented. To invent the lever, a genius was needed, and indeed, all the fallen apes must have been geniuses. If not, they could not have survived a situation for which they were unfit. We, the victims of demographic inflation, can no longer imagine such an aristocratic vision of the human being. § Now consider this hairy ape, that aristocratic genius, as he lies there, flat on his back, and attempts to get up. You should not compare him to a newborn baby, because there are transcendent parental arms that help the baby get up and slowly, painfully, after several months, become *Homo erectus*. No transcendental arms float over the fallen ape; his simian parents have hidden in the receding treetops. Instead, one should compare him to a fallen beetle. However, the ape does not flail with six legs, as the beetle does, but with two legs and two arms, each equipped with a curious five-legged spider. It is these spiders which are the saviours of the fallen ape and they, the human hands, which merit closer examination where human history and the invention of the lever are concerned. § As the fallen anthropoid — two million years ago over there in East Africa — is trying desperately to get to his feet (which are not made to support his heavy body), his two hands scan the surface of the ground upon which he fell. They feel around, they touch, they grasp, they hold, they manipulate, they rotate the objects they grasp and hold. These two surrealistic five-legged spiders have been executing complex gestures ever since. They have scanned our surroundings and the result is what we call civilisation. Every motion in each complex gesture has been submitted to scrutiny and a catalogue of these motions has been repeatedly proposed. For instance: perception, conception, understanding, evaluation, and production. The remarkable thing about this dance of the hands within the world is that it is unlike all other animal motions. Take, for example, a normal, eight-legged spider. It sits within its web and waits for something to happen. If something hits the web, it executes a motion. But this something which hits the web (and thus elicits the spider's attention) must fall within one of three types: it must be edible, copulable, or dangerous. If it is none of these, the spider will not take action. The same applies for simian hands, which are so similar to our own: they extend to grasp food, a sexual partner, or to avoid danger (for instance, holding fast to branches). But our hands function the opposite way. They extend to grasp mostly objects of a fourth type, which cannot be eaten, copulated with, or which represent any danger, such as stones lying on the ground or sticks broken from branches. Our hands are Kantian in the sense that, as Kant said, beauty is that which pleases without being interesting. Our hands execute disinterested motions. The fallen anthropoid demonstrates why: out of desperation. § You may object that young animals play, and thus execute similar gestures. But this objection is not valid. Take this example: the fallen anthropoid feels, touches, grasps, holds on to and manipulates a stick, rotating it and using it as a lever to lift himself into an upright position. This may be stated in a different manner: he understands that sticks ought to be levers and then he evaluates the stick and realises the lever. To be sure, the fallen anthropoid plays like other young animals. But while doing so he differentiates between what is and what ought to be, between the real and values, thus creating the sciences and culture. To get on his feet, the fallen anthropoid must play with his hands and produce a lever — which is to say, he must produce scientific knowledge and artistic values. § This phenomenological description of the Origin of Man and of Human history, in general, has taken the lever as its point of departure. It is thus a mechanistic vision of humanity and of culture. But before you condemn such an attitude as being too simplistic, consider the principle on which the lever stands: before we can use the lever, we must find a point of support. That point cannot itself be part of mechanics. It must be, necessarily, trans-mechanics. This is true of every approach to the Origin of what we are: it will eventually bump up against something which transcends it. This is probably because our Origin is not located in a specific space, be it Platonic ideas, Paradise, or treetops. There is something out-of-space, utopic, about us. Look at a lever and you shall see it. *

AN IMPROBABLE STORY

Originally unpublished

§ Literature: a term that means a "set of letters." The story begins about 3,500 years ago and appears to be approaching an end. This is why we must hurry if we want to tell the story. Once literature is finished, nothing can be told, even the story of literature itself. When there are no more letters, people will illustrate or calculate the world – not describe it. But even before letters disappear, telling literature's story poses a problem. The description of literature itself is a part of literature, and a text which recounts the end of the story is a tale that devours its own body. It is the complement to Ouroboros, that tail-devouring serpent.

§ About 3,500 years ago, some people on the eastern shores of the Mediterranean made the following proposal: from now on, certain signs which have so far meant words shall mean the sound with which these words begin. Thus, the sign "aleph," which has thus far meant the word "bull," shall mean the Semitic sound "a" with which the word "aleph" (bull) begins. Or: the sign "beth," which thus far has meant the word "house," shall now mean the sound "b" with which the word "beth" (house) begins. This proposal was accepted by a few merchants and priests who began to process the newly convened letters and therefore may be called "*literati*" or "*hommes de lettres.*" § Western culture has been satisfied with 26 letters, which is a modest amount and does not seem to pose problems for processing. But beware: letters are types, not characters, and although there are only 26 prototypes, countless stereotypes inundate the land and demand constant processing. These stereotypes are unevenly distributed: "e's" and "a's" can be found everywhere, but there are regions where "x's" and "w's" are rare. The frequency of letters in specific regions may be calculated, and this constitutes a quantified critique of literature. However, this manner of critique has its limits. Usually literature is not produced by the method of random letter distribution. § Those who process letters do so in an orderly fashion. Their purpose is to visualise the sounds of a spoken language and transcode language from sound into image. By doing so the *literati* introduced a barrier between the text and its writer. The writer could no longer directly transcribe his thoughts; they had to pass through a language. This complication became unavoidable if one wanted to preserve oral communication in the era before the invention of letters, records, and magnetic tape. § He who processes letters has to adhere to the rules of language. It soon appeared that these rules, when applied consistently, reformulated the very languages from which they were abstracted. The result was literally language. Additionally, it appeared that more rules were necessary for orderly language transcription. When applied in a disciplined manner, these overlapping sets of rules, such as grammar and orthography, would result in a group of letters called "text," which means the "fabric" of letters. § The sources of literature are meagre, and the texts that stem from them few and precious. But as the story proceeds, texts multiply, thanks to mutually reinforcing methods. Each text might produce several new ones and the new texts intersect and fertilise one another. Each text splits and divides, spreading its own life.

Over time, each divided text could unite with any other, and incorporate, reintegrate, and disintegrate into numerous texts. This web of letters formed like an avalanche and expanded in every direction. It broadened, visualising one language after another. It widened, submitting successively new regions of thought and experience into the code of letters. It grew upward, advancing into an increasingly refined articulation of thought, feeling, and decision. After the invention of the printing press, it advanced into more private corners in common people's daily lives. This high tide of letters began to inundate all continents, mostly in the form of printed matter. It devoured an immense quantity of paper. It devastated forests. No one could protect him- or herself from its mind-polluting effects. An uninterrupted flood of sperm flows from the male organs of humanity into the female organs, producing future processors and consumers of letters. Billions of people are now immersed in trillions of letters, at risk of drowning. § But this is not a full assessment of the catastrophe. The fact is, texts, which multiply, cross, overlap, and mutually devour one another, are equipped with sticky threads and cling to each other. These threads binding letters together form lumps on multiple levels: grammar, linguistic rhythm, and the design of lines and pages. Sticky filaments link texts on conscious, semiconscious, and unconscious levels, creating unsuspected connections between texts that seemingly reside far afield. These connections preserve the meanings of words, the vibrations of sentences, and style. This stickiness of literature nurtures our incapacity to think for ourselves, to formulate a thought on our own. Every time we believe we have a novel thought, we find that we have read it somewhere else. The thousands and thousands of sticky threads connecting the texts extend beyond our memories to texts we haven't read, which nonetheless influence us. To our despair, we have to admit that we are prisoners in this web of texts, like flies in a spider's web. Like flies, we struggle in vain to be free from the sticky filaments that bind us. § In the course of centuries, this improbable flood of letters has engulfed us like a malign spirit casting a spell with an aim to destroy us. In the beginning, texts were weak and had to overcome images, which had been the bearers of communication before the invention of letters. Later, in the Renaissance, when texts seemed victorious, it was found that numbers were better suited to formulate discoveries in the natural sciences and the code of letters was considered, comparatively, imprecise. In the 19th-century, photographs and other technical images were invented and these images — especially television — became increasingly more important as bearers of communication. Later, records, tape recorders, and other technical methods were invented to transcode and store oral communication and letters became obsolete as a method for visually coding language. What is apparent for a critic of culture is that this is the current state of letters.

§ On the mass-communications level, moving and speaking images are far more efficient than letters. On the level of scientific communication, algorithms are far more precise than letters. On the level of decision-making and programming, computer codes are far more efficient than letters. As a method of storing and visualising spoken language, letters were superseded long ago by more advanced technical apparatus like records or magnetic tape. For all of these complementary and convergent reasons, letters should be abandoned and literature should be over and done with. § What we observe, however, is a quite different situation. Texts continue to multiply and depreciate in unparalleled fashion. No sooner do we throw out unopened mail and our mailbox is full again with this kind of rubbish. How can this letter-catastrophe undermining the very foundations of civilisation be explained? How did we become attached to this unreasonable mass of letters? Why do we prefer to drown in letters instead of liberating ourselves from them? Here is one explanation: there must be a book somewhere on a shelf in some library which contains everything we seek; all the wisdom, beauty, and goodness of which we have dreamed. It must be contained in this book, if only we could find it. This book must exist somewhere. Because, if we have been processing letters for 3,500 years, someone must have written it. Maybe it is an Armenian book, written in the 13th-century and hidden in the Caucasus. Or perhaps it is a book in a not-yet-invented language, written in the 45th-century and hidden somewhere in the Antarctic region. In the vast letter-flood, such a book, a stone of wisdom, must be hidden somewhere — for the same reason that, if chimpanzees type for a million years, they must, of necessity, eventually write *The Divine Comedy*. It is this hope against hope, this reasoning against reason that makes us believe literature is the preferred method for attaining wisdom, and which explains why we continue to write and read, even though we ought to know better. *

BACKLASH

Originally unpublished

§ We make tools, they strike back. This establishes the structure of civilisation. For instance: We create levers by simulating the capacity of our arms to lift an inanimate object. The lever strikes back, and we now move our arms as if they were levers. Or: We breed sheep by simulating in an animate object the capacity of our breasts to secrete milk. The sheep strikes back, and we now behave like sheep, needing "spiritual" shepherds such as bishops and pastors. We simulate our own simulations. This backlash is growing virulently at the moment: youngsters dance as if they were robots; bank tellers behave like automata; scientists think like computers; and artists act like data plotters. This structure begs the following description concerning the history of civilisation: in Palaeolithic times, people hunted with tools such as stone knives and jackals they tamed and trained to help them hunt. The knives were simulations of teeth, the jackals were simulations of legs, and people behaved like knives and jackals. This sort of behaviour was called "magic." In

Neolithic times, people worked with tools such as ploughs and oxen. The ploughs simulated toes, the oxen simulated muscles, and people behaved like ploughs and oxen. This sort of behaviour was called "myth." In the Bronze Age, people used tools such as swords and horses. The swords were simulations of knives, the horses simulated oxen, and people behaved like swords and horses. This sort of behaviour was called "heroic." In the Iron Age, people used tools like bars and wires. The bars were simulations of bones, the wires simulated nerves, and people behaved like bones and nerves. This sort of behaviour was called "scientific." Instead of trying to analyse what is meant by magic, myth, heroism, and scientific organisation, we should analyse the backlash of our tools. If we did so, we might program the future. When building future tools, we might program into them the backlash they will exert upon us.

§ History has been a blind process so far because no one considered the effect tools have upon humans. Stone knives were not made for performing magic dances, and wires were not made for disproving the theories of Newton. In fact, it is difficult to foresee how a tool will strike back against its user. Take an example: ploughs required people to build permanent homes, which led to villages and political life, which resulted in political parties. But who could have foreseen that ploughs would strike back against people in the form of political parties? Such futurisation has become possible at present, however, because tool making is changing. § The first change occurred during the industrial revolution. Tools were no longer made empirically, according to traditional models, but on the basis of scientific research. This explains why animals (animated tools) became obsolete: there were no scientific theories permitting the industrial production of jackals or oxen. Animate tools are more clever than inanimate ones (an ox is more intelligent than a plough), but they are mortal. This is why our behaviour became more mechanical and less intelligent during the industrial revolution: we simulated machines instead of jackals. But this is about to change: now we have scientific theories in biology and more intelligent tools are in the making. § We are beginning to build levers equipped with simulations of our nervous system (artificial intelligence), and soon we will be building artificial jackals and oxen, using genetic manipulation. This will be the second industrial revolution and it will render inanimate machines obsolete, just as the first one rendered horses obsolete. These tools will strike back at us and in the future we will behave less mechanically and more intelligently. We will simulate our simulated intelligence. But this is not what is so revolutionary about the second industrial revolution. It will allow us to program the backlash of tools and include in that program the design of future tools. History will become a deliberate process. § Tools are objects designed to "work," which means to pluck pieces out of the world, change their shape, and place them where we are (at our disposal). This is what the word "production" means — namely, to guide parts of the world (*pro-ducere*) from where they are to where they should be. This action of tools is called "their economic function." During most of history, tools were designed with this view in mind. Lately, it has become obvious that plucking pieces from the world changes the whole world. This aspect of tools is called "their ecological function." Lately, ecological considerations have been taken into account in the course of designing tools. Now it is becoming painfully obvious that tools strike back at us. This aspect of tools may be called "their anthropological function," and it will become possible and necessary to design them, taking this function into account. § This will imply a profound change of attitude in the face of civilisation, which can be illustrated by the following example: in Neolithic times it became necessary to build structures to shelter the harvest. These "public buildings" were constructed on trash heaps that accumulated near villages, in order to protect the harvest from being inundated. A guardian was appointed to watch over the storehouse. This guardian collected the harvest and distributed it in the winter. He evolved into a Big Man, and later into a priest, a king, and into God himself in Heaven. The trash heap evolved into a tower, the Kremlin and the White House. Moreover, from where the guardian sat he could see the course of the local river and thus program canal building. This was the beginning of geometry and modern science. The harvest-shelter was originally a tool designed for economic reasons. Its anthropological function (the way it struck back against its users) was political, religious, and scientific. Nothing of this was programmed into the design of the shelter, which shows how history has been a blind process, thus far. Now we are challenged to design future shelters with a view to the political, religious, and scientific backlash they will exert upon us.

§ In designing the intelligent tools of the future, we will have to know how we want them to strike back at us, and this implies that we will have to know how we want to change in the future. It is commonplace to say that we change the world in order to change ourselves, but now this adage is becoming a technical problem. The design of humanity's shape is the challenge.

§ This is a formidable challenge. It supposes that we not only know how we want to be in the future, but also that we agree about this amongst ourselves. There are very few signs, so far, that suggest humanity's ability to take responsibility for its own destiny, and design it. But it cannot be avoided. If we continue to design our tools based on economic and ecological considerations alone, and continue to disregard anthropological considerations, there is no doubt that civilisation will smother us; tools will strike back and transform us into an amorphous jelly. Because, as the tools become ever more intelligent, they become more powerful than us. The only way to restrain the tools is to design them for their anthropological functions. We have to decide how we want to be, and agree amongst ourselves, or it will be the end of human civilisation. Either history will become a deliberate process or there will be no history in the future.

§ This is a radical statement. But the situation we are in is a radically new one. Our tools are striking back at us in a way we can no longer tolerate, if we want to survive as human beings — not only the tools designed to destroy humans (like nuclear weapons), but tools that were designed to serve humans (like computers). To utter this is to be optimistic about the future. People have always stood up to challenges that were strong enough to threaten their existence. They might do it again and thus, for the first time in history, shape their own destinies by designing a civilisation that strikes back in the form of a more meaningful human existence. *

BIBLIOPHAGUS CONVICTUS

Originally unpublished

§ The recent discovery of a new species of insect of the order *Hymenoptera* is remarkable, both in itself and in the way it was discovered. The insect stores printed information in the collective memory of its hive, and it was discovered in the brain of a writer. Of course: scientific progress has made us accustomed to take new discoveries in stride, without paying much attention to them. Still: this one should be noted.

§ Although the classification *Bibliophagus convictus* does pose a few taxonomic problems, it is undoubtedly a kind of bee, and it could be mistaken for one, if it weren't for its unusual antennae. When not feeding or communicating, it wraps itself up in these antennae, which make it look like a speck of dirt on the page, to be brushed away while reading. This also explains why it escaped attention for so long. (The reader unfamiliar with the biology of *Hymenoptera* in general, and of bees in particular, should consult the article "Insects" in the *Encyclopædia Britannica* — although *Bibliophagus convictus* is not mentioned there yet.) One peculiarity of the species is that it feeds exclusively on printed matter: when offered a handwritten manuscript or a teletext, it will refuse. Another peculiarity is that it refuses any text that has been previously eaten by another *Bibliophagus*, even if that text was a different edition or in a different language. The physiological explanation for this oddity is that, after devouring a paragraph (*Bibliophagus* never eats single lines or entire pages), the insect ruminates and secretes an enzyme called "criticase," which reacts with the printer's ink to form an acid called "informasis." This morsel is then rolled around in the insect's mouth until it forms a ball, which is vomited into the mouth of another *Bibliophagus*. The process of criticase secretion, informasis formation, and mouth-to-mouth transmission is repeated until all the members of the hive have chewed on this particular bit of informasis. A messenger (called the "mediator") is then sent to the next hive with the bit of informasis in his mouth, and a chain is formed which links all the *Bibliophagi* hives in the world. During this process, parts of the chewed informasis are swallowed, entering the digestive apparatus, and processed in typical insect fashion (much like pollen). In the queen, however, informasis penetrates the ovaries and infiltrates the genetic information. Thus, each new text will result in a mutation of the entire species when devoured by any *Bibliophagus*. This is why a "second reading" will result in cancerous growth within the genetic matter: "redundancy." This poses a problem: the insertion of quotations from old texts into new ones endangers the species and threatens degeneration. § This is not the most serious threat to the species' survival, however. Statistics show that the growth of the *Bibliophagus* population exceeds that of printed texts, despite the current increase in their numbers. Extending the two curves, *Bibliophagus* population and printed texts, into the next two decades, one can see that the species is approaching extinction, due to a lack of food. Initial cases of *Bibliophagus* cannibalism (a symptom of species extinction) have been observed. However, there are other indicators that suggest the species' capacity to adapt to adverse conditions: a rather obscure writer was found dead in his apartment, all evidence pointing to suicide by poison. And yet, the police were struck by the fact the dead man had written an article condemning suicide, and that article was found in manuscript form lying next to the body. The police ordered an autopsy, which revealed an anomaly in the writer's brain and, on closer examination, a living *Bibliophagus*. This is how the species was discovered. It was soon obvious that the poison that killed the man was informasis, secreted by the insect . The puzzle police had to solve was how the insect had gotten into the writer's brain. This question was answered when it was discovered that the victim had undergone trepanation. The surgeon who performed the operation told the police (rather reluctantly) that there was no clinical justification for the procedure: the patient had solicited it and offered the surgeon a considerable sum of money. The only explanation was that the insect had convinced the writer to have his skull opened, to allow *Bibliophagus* to enter his brain. Further investigation showed that this trepanation was not an isolated case, but part of an epidemic spreading from

Manhattan to London and Paris, and currently centred in the Frankfurt Book Fair. Most of the trepanation subjects refused to testify, until one, a dissident Catholic theologian, agreed to tell his story. While reading his Bible, the theologian encountered a *Bibliophagus* crawling along a line in the text that stated, It is not good for man to be alone. The insect was quite obviously signalling to him with its antennae. The theologian, who was versed in deciphering difficult Chaldean and Ugaritic codes, was able to discern its gestures. A dialogue between himself and the insect was established. The theologian mimicked the motions of the antennae with his fingertips, eventually leading to trepanation and the insect implanted in his brain. The man refused to disclose the substance of the dialogue, however, for two reasons: first, he claimed that his entire testimony was not really his own, but that of *Bibliophagus*; second, he insisted in calling the insect "the Devil" instead of *Bibliophagus*. That man has now been committed to an asylum.

§ Another important step in the investigation occurred when a correlation between *Bibliophagus* population growth and the trepanation epidemic was discovered. Computers calculated a chance probability of one in fifteen thousand. Thus, we have to assume, as a working hypothesis, that the epidemic is a symptom of the *Bibliophagus* species' attempt to survive by increasing writers' production. This hypothesis may also throw light on the present cultural situation, explaining the proliferation of new texts at the moment. § Printing texts is no longer useful: there are better ways to distribute information. Alphabetically coded texts are easier to distribute and store as teletexts than as printed matter. The alphabet itself is no longer a useful code; digital codes are more efficient. And when it comes to articulating, distributing, and storing complex information, audiovisual images such as videos and synthetic computer images are better than linear notation. Thus, the fact that texts continue to be printed (and their number is increasing) is a mystery — unless we explain it by the active presence of *Bibliophagus* within the printing process. § However, it is not sufficient to assume that writers of printable manuscripts and publishers themselves are carriers of *Bibliophagi*. It must be admitted that *Bibliophagus'* dissemination is much broader. The uselessness of printing is so rarely discussed it constitutes a conspiracy to silence the problem, and this conspiracy points to the widespread contamination of society by informasis. It may even be claimed that, in the so-called "developed" countries, each and every human brain contains a *Bibliophagus* that goes undetected, due to informasis secretion. Systematic blood testing of the entire population, to measure informasis levels, should be required. § The problem of parasitism will be central to future analyses of culture. At first glance, the symbiosis "*Homo sapiens-Bibliophagus convictus*" looks like a case of insects parasitizing the human body. However, this will not hold up under investigation. A better interpretation of the phenomenon is that the printing press was invented with the purpose to feed *Bibliophagus*. The first brain implanted with *Bibliophagus* was Gutenberg's, and all subsequent writers and publishers have been influenced by *Bibliophagus'* secretions. Thus, it appears that all modern literature is a case of the human mind parasitizing an insect. It should be kept in mind, however, that this interpretation itself was inspired by a *Bibliophagus* implanted in the brain of the man who wrote this article. *

WHY MAKE CHILDREN

Originally unpublished

§ There is a biological answer to this question: because life tends toward multiplication. It arose a relatively short time ago (some four billion years), creeping onto beaches where the atmosphere, the hydrosphere, and the geosphere mingled. Life's tendency was to establish a biosphere by penetrating the three existing spheres and wrapping itself around the planet. Now the biomass is not an amorphous liquid, like seawater, which spreads simply by increasing its volume. Instead, it is a viscous mass composed of tiny droplets, each containing a complex nucleus carrying the program for spreading life. The biomass can only increase through the division of the droplets that constitute it. Or, instead of "division," one may say "section." Life can only spread by sectioning, or "sex." Thus, the biological answer to our question is that we make children because of sex, which is the biomass' method for increasing itself.

§ But this is obviously an unsatisfactory answer. We do not make children by splitting. The greater part of the biomass (the "protozoa") does so, but humanity does not. Humanity belongs to that lesser portion of the biomass for which sex is a more complicated matter. For this lesser portion, two droplets mingle before they split, which sounds like an absurd idea. But it has its logic. When a droplet divides, the program it contains cannot be divided too, because that would result in a progressive elimination of that program. The program must be copied so that each droplet itself contains a full program. However, in the process of copying, many mistakes occur. Arid life "degenerates" — meaning, the "genetic information" (program) de-forms. This apparently absurd strategy, to have two droplets mingle before dividing, is meant to limit the number of copying mistakes, and hence avoid degeneration. This is the origin of the famous (or infamous) "two sexes." § There is a further complication, though. In "metazoa" such as ourselves — that is, lumps in the biomass where droplets (cells) assemble — it is not two bodies that mingle before dividing. Instead, each body contains specialised cells that are meant to mingle with equally specialised cells from another body. This is even more absurd, because the bodies ("organisms"), with all their complex functions and problems, have the sole purpose of transporting these specialised cells in order to mingle and divide. The complex organisms ("living beings") are essentially nothing but redundant protuberances that emerge from the biomass, secrete these specialised cells, plunge back into the biomass, and disappear from view. This emergence is called "birth." The plunging back into the biomass is called "death," and this process has very little to do with the tendency toward life increasing on the planet. Life is not concerned with living beings – with their births, biographies, or deaths. It is only concerned with the specialised cells secreted by living beings. To put this more elegantly: life is not concerned with "phenotypes" (living beings) but with "genotypes" (specialised cells that mingle and divide). To put this briefly: life does not like us. We are an accident in biological evolution. § Life does not care whether or not we die, as long as we make children (secrete cells that mingle with other cells). But we care. Although life does not like us, we like it. Our unrequited love does not suit life. It wants us to make children (as many as possible) and die (as quickly as possible). But we refuse to do so. We even refuse to make children when it puts our own lives in danger. This is why life devised a further strategy to seduce us into making children: orgasm. It wants us to make children, even if we run the risk of dying in the process. Orgasm is the best strategy devised by life so far in its struggle against living beings. But of course: we humans are more clever than life. § We like to live and we like orgasm, but we do not like making children when it involves danger. So we invented a way to separate orgasm from making children. For example, pills and abortions. Long live life (let us live long), long live orgasm (let us have as much of it as possible), and down with the dangerous making of children. Sex thus no longer serves as the means of multiplying life, but instead improving the quality of life (meaning: ours). But there is a curious aspect to orgasm that requires consideration. It is meant to make us forget about death while making children. But he who says "forget about death" is saying "forget about yourself." Orgasm makes us selfless. In orgasm, two people forget about themselves and merge with one another. This is not in life's program. (It used to be called "love," but this word can no longer be used because it's kitschy and sticks to the tongue the moment one utters it.) This is not in life's program, because it does nothing to advance life's tendency to increase. This selflessness shows how we humans may overcome our biological condition. "*Omnia vincit amor*," the Ancients said. § Thus, the biological answer to our question "Why make children?" is not a sufficient one. There is a better answer. We make children to carry on the struggle against our biological condition. For us, a child is not the bearer of genetic information received on some ancient beach, which he is destined to transmit to some unimaginable future organisms. For us, a child is the bearer of cultural information in the elaboration of which we also collaborated, and which he is destined to enrich with his own contribution. We make children not for sexual but for cultural reasons. Therefore, the making of children only became a human commitment after its separation from sex and the invention of pills and abortions. § The artificial (meaning: really human) methods for making children are only in their first stages. It has already become possible to deposit sperm in a bank, and virgins may withdraw the sperm they want and fertilise their eggs. Soon, society will be full of such virgins, created by immaculate conception. And these virgins will, of course, indulge in multiple orgasms for the sheer pleasure of it. Soon, sperm and eggs will be collected from humans and mingled in specialised apparatus, and artificial uteruses will bring forth well-bred children. This will be the final liberation of women. Children will then become biological hardware for cultural software and humanity will become emancipated from childbearing, for childcare. A truly "pedagogical" humanity will have come about, one that has overcome its biological condition. § But before we embrace this luminous utopia, a word of caution. If orgasm becomes independent from multiplication (from "sex"), if it becomes *"l'art pour l'art,"* will it not lose an important feature? If two people forget themselves and become one in orgasm and nothing results from it (no child), is there a danger of irresponsibility? And conversely: if children are born from artifice (and not mutual selflessness), will they be loved the way children born the old way are loved? These are reactionary objections, of course, and they smell of ancient prejudices. But they merit consideration. Because, to be fully human is not only to overcome our biological condition, but to lift that condition to a human level, which is what "overcome" really means: to do away with it by ascending to a higher level. *

ON BRANCHES AND STICKS, OR, WHAT IS FREEDOM GOOD FOR?

Originally unpublished

§ If a deer walks in the forest, it is the forest moving, like leaves in the wind. The forest is a complex system of movements (an "ecosystem"). But if a man walks in the forest, his movement disturbs that complex system: it is input. This may be shown by the following example: the man breaks off a branch that stands in his way and he uses it to break other branches. He tears an object from its context (he "produces" it) and turns it against its context (he applies it). This typically human gesture is called "art," and it has an obvious purpose: to clear a pathway in the forest. How are we to interpret this? § One way is this: man does not dwell in the forest like deer; instead, he inhabits an abyss between two worlds. One world is as it is, but not as it should be (for instance: the forest). The other should be, but is not (the world of values). The branch is, but not as it should be, because it stands in the way (in Greek: it is a "problem"). The stick should be, but before I produce it, it is not; it is an unrealised value (in Greek: it is an "ideal"). Art is a method for solving problems and realising values: the stick I produce is a branch, as it should be. The stick is an artefact, an artifice, and a work of art. § By opposing "what ought to be" with "what is," man negates what is. In fact, his very existence is that negation. This negation used to be called "spirit." There are people who do not like that negation and do not like themselves: they prefer branches to sticks and forests to the exploitation of forests. They would like to walk in the forest like deer. However, such a double negation will not transform them into deer: ecologists, green activists, and mystics are failed deer. This must be said. And yet, having said that, it must be admitted that sticks are not very good at opening pathways. Are we freer to walk than we were before we began producing sticks? Do cave bears and hailstorms oppress us more than the secret police and thermonuclear weapons? Is art a good method for opening pathways for the "spirit"? § The answer is no, because the stick can obstruct one's way at least as much as the branch. It may have been placed there on purpose. This is not the fault of art (or its younger brother, technology) but of evil people (capitalists and/or communists) who are to blame for misusing it. But this is not a good excuse for art either: if it is a method for achieving freedom, how can it be abused? There must be some intrinsic contradiction within art itself that allows for this abuse. § It is easy to see this contradiction: the stick, even though it is an object torn from its original context, is still an object. Which is to say, we are still subjected to it, and we are subjected to it in a more complex manner than we are to branches. The fact is, the stick strikes back at the stick producer, who strikes back at the stick – until a Gordian knot of feedback makes it impossible to distinguish between the stick and its producer. To illustrate this knot binding us to the object, let us consider a few instances of feedback. I break off a branch and this allows me to see what the branch is like: I have gained knowledge. I turn the branch around and this allows me to see how sticks ought to be; I have gained insight into values. Then I use the stick as a sort of third leg and this allows me to see how legs work: I have gained self-knowledge. As I walk with my stick, I do it better than before: I have changed my behaviour. Having seen the stick as a sort of leg, I can make a better stick next time. And having seen that the leg is a sort of stick, I can walk better next time. Thus, art is a source of knowledge, of (political and aesthetic) evaluation, and of self-knowledge; it changes the world and it changes man, but it establishes man's dependence upon sticks (culture).

§ This concrete experience, with increasing knowledge, deeper insight into values, and better self-knowledge — and which accompanies stick production (artistic gesture) — is a fascinating, inebriating adventure. It absorbs me. It is as if a voice within the branch had called me, saying: "I dare you to turn me around." And I had followed that calling like a vocation. I became the victim of a giddiness ("vertiginous creativity"), which made me forget why I wanted to create the stick in the first place. I no longer make sticks in order to open up pathways (for freedom), but in order to make ever more perfect sticks; to become a greater stick producer. (The universe of artificial objects that surrounds us is the result of that giddiness, that oblivion of what art is for.) § When I walk in the forest, I do not do so in the abstract. Instead, I enter it, coming from a specific historical cultural situation which has programmed me to believe that branches ought to be sticks, and equipped with methods on how to make them. Generations of stick producers have entered the forest before me, and I carry them with me. When I turn my own branch into a stick, it is those generations within me who do so, and the stick I produce is the last link in an immemorial stick tradition. All the previous stick producers and all the sticks ever produced are somehow here with me now. Although the producers are dead and the sticks have decayed, they are immortal within me. And I will be immortal, and so will the stick I produce, if only I hand my stick over to the next stick producer, and my stick is slightly different from all the previous ones, so that the next producer can distinguish and remember it. Thus, stick production becomes an attempt to overcome death and become immortal. Or, to put it less selfishly, to live for others and to live on within them. Now, if stick production gives meaning to my life, which extends beyond my death, how can I to remember that I started making sticks merely in order to open a pathway in the forest? § The Gordian knot that binds the artist to his stick binds the stick's user equally, only differently. Thus, man becomes a subject to his artefacts even more than to natural objects. The original purpose of art (to free us from objects) has fallen into oblivion. And yet, suddenly technology (that most sophisticated art) seems to cut this Gordian knot and deliver us from our subjectivity to objects. If this were not actually happening, it would strike us as utterly fantastic. Technology achieves this marvel with two artifices: "automation" and "immaterial information." This is how art will look in the immediate future: I will no longer need to tear a branch from a tree and turn it around to become a stick: a robot will do this for me. What I will have to do is program the robot to perform this operation. And I will do so by synthesizing an image of the stick on a computer screen and feeding the image to the robot. Thus, art will no longer be concerned with changing the world so that it may become as it should be (the robot does that better). It will be concerned with instructing the robot on how the world should be (with the manipulation of values). No longer will man have to face objects and their perfidious inertia (the robot will do that). Man will no longer be subject to objects. Instead, he will manipulate values (models, ideals) and the values elaborated will be automatically realised. Is this not "absolute" freedom, in the truest sense of the term: "ab-solute," namely "ab-stracted" from objects? And in this, has not art finally found its way back to its original purpose? Thanks to art and technology, are we on the threshold of freedom? § Yes, but with this question: Why should the robot make sticks if it is the robot and not ourselves who enters the forest? Are the sticks-to-be, which the artist synthesises on his screen, meant to open pathways for robots? What good are they? What good is freedom? (By the way, this question is characteristic of freedom achieved: no longer "free from something," but "free to do something"). The question amounts to this: what is art going to do (what are we going to do, since apparently everybody is going to be an artist) if art no longer has to face objects? § There is an obvious answer: images of sticks-to-be will be made for the pure pleasure of image-making. *"Ars gratia artis."* But this *"art pour l'art"* answer cannot be a good one, because it is the essence of the stick-to-be that a branch ought to be like it, too. It is the essence of the stick-to-be that is meant to give a meaning to branches. Thus, the second and more complicated answer to this question is that the business of an art set free from objective resistance is to create meaning (*"Sinngebung"*) - which has been its business from the beginning, except that this was obscured by art's involvement with objects. "What is the meaning of a branch? It is meant to be a stick." "What is the meaning of a bull in Lascaux? It is meant to be hunted." The business of art is to impose meanings on the world, which is absurdly as it is, and thus to create meaning for human existence. Art set free from objective resistance will be free to pursue its own business. This is what freedom is good for.

§ But all of this is utter cynical nonsense. Most people are in no position to ask what freedom is good for. They are oppressed by hunger, disease, and brutal tyranny, and they may be relied upon to prevent us from playing around with robots and computers. Once they are able to transform a branch into a stick, they will use it to break our screens (and our heads, should we be sitting in front of them). And they will be doing this earlier and better, if we use our screens to design the sticks for them. So this whole utopian vision of an art, set free to create meaning, may be seen as a symptom of decadence: we use our newly won freedom to commit suicide. § It will be noted that this paper has avoided, out of prudishness, the word "alienation." It can no longer avoid it. Art's involvement with objects was a method for overcoming alienation. In turning a branch around, man attempted to overcome his alienation from the forest. Automation, by freeing art from branches, has deprived art of its "work-therapeutic" dimension — all those fascinating and inebriating aspects that were discussed when the Gordian knot was being untangled. Art set free in this way throws man back into total alienation. Not being subject to objects, man is no longer a subject, in any sense of that term. Our children and grandchildren sitting in front of their terminals, synthesizing sticks-to-be, are the very image of alienation. Hungry and persecuted children will tolerate this image. Which obliges us to conclude that absolute freedom is synonymous with total alienation. Therefore, this paper wants to be read as a paean to absolute freedom, to total alienation. Or, to put it into historical perspective: a paean to folly. *

ON BEING SUBJECT TO OBJECTS

Originally unpublished

§ Man, unlike all other known living beings, does not dwell in the world. He is an intruder. This may be shown by the following example: if a deer walks in the forest, its movement is motion of the forest itself, like the movement of leaves in the wind, or birds in the branches. If a man walks in the forest, however, his movement disturbs the complex system of motion (the "ecosystem"), which is the forest. He breaks off a branch that stands in his way, turns it around, and uses it as a stick to break off further branches. He tears an object from its context (he "pro-duces" it), and he uses it to advance against its original context (he "applies" it). This typically human gesture, transforming branches into sticks (nature into culture), this technical and/or artistic gesture, has an obvious purpose: to clear a path in the forest (to open a space for freedom). But understanding this gesture is not as simple. § This is a way of understanding it: man lives in the abyss between two worlds. One is as it is, but not as it should be (the phenomenal world, where all other living beings live). The other should be, but is not (the world of values). For man, to live is to attempt to bring these two worlds together so that the world that is can be as it should be, and the world that should be can be. Before man entered the forest, the branch was not as it should be: it stood in the way - or, in Greek, it was a "problem." The stick is how the branch should be. And before man entered the forest, the stick did not exist; it was an "unrealised value." Technology and the arts are methods for solving problems and realising values. The stick is a problem solved, a realised value. It permits man to climb out of his abyss. (To put it more elegantly: the stick overcomes human alienation.) § By opposing "ought to be" with "being," man negates everything that is as it is: his entire existence is this negation (which used to be called "spirit"). There are, of course, people who do not like this negation (which defines them), and who prefer branches to sticks and forests to forest exploitation. They would like to walk in the forest like deer. They deny "spirit." This double negation does not result in ecologists, green activists, and other romantics and mystics becoming deer. And yet, one must admit that sticks and their corollaries do not necessarily make us free; they do not necessarily open spaces for freedom. Are we more free than we were before we began producing sticks? Do cave bears and hailstorms oppress us more than the secret police and thermonuclear weapons? Are technology and the arts good methods for the world to become as it is, or as it should be? Are they good methods for opening pathways for the "spirit"?

§ The answer is no, because the stick may stand in one's way as much as the branch — only more so. It may stand in one's way because it was placed there on purpose. We may be oppressed by culture on a higher level than we were by nature. It may be said that this is not the fault of technology and the arts, but of evil people like capitalists and/or communists, who abuse them. This is not a very good excuse, however, for the following reason: if the purpose of technology and the arts is to make us more free, how is it possible to abuse them? There must be some intrinsic contradiction in technology and the arts which permits this abuse. § This contradiction may be easily stated: the stick, although it is an object torn from its original context and turned around, is still an object. Which is to say, we are still subject to it. We are "conditioned" by it, and in a very complicated fashion — much more than we are conditioned by branches. The stick strikes back at its producer, who strikes back at the stick, until a Gordian knot of feedback relations makes it impossible to distinguish between the stick and the producer. § To illustrate, let us consider a few examples of feedback. I break off a branch and this allows me to see a branch better: I have gained knowledge. Then I turn the branch around and this allows me to see how a stick should be: I have gained insight into values. Then I use the stick as a kind of third arm (or leg) and this allows me to see how arms and legs work: I have gained self-knowledge. As I walk with my stick in hand, I do it better than I did before: I have changed my behaviour. Having thus learned that sticks can function as a sort of leg, and legs like sticks, I can create better sticks next time —

and this allows me to use my legs even better. To put this a little more elegantly, the production of cultural objects changes nature, man, and culture, and establishes man's dependence on culture. It is also the source of knowledge (science) and changes political and aesthetic values.

§ This concrete experience of increasing knowledge, self-knowledge, and deeper insight into values, which accompanies stick production, is a fascinating, inebriating adventure. It may enthral me. It is as if a voice called from within the branch, saying, "I dare you to turn me around," and I followed that calling, that vocation. I became the victim of a creative giddiness, of vertiginous creativity, which made me forget why I wanted to make the stick in the first place. I no longer make sticks in order to open pathways in the forest, but to make increasingly better sticks and to become a perfect stick producer. The technological and artistic universe that surrounds us is a result of this giddiness, of this oblivion to its original purpose. § But, of course, when I enter the forest, it is not an abstraction, but a specific historical situation. I enter the forest from cultural surroundings which have programmed me to believe branches ought to be sticks, and with knowledge of how to make them. Generations of stick producers have entered the forest before me and I carry them with me. When I turn my own branch into a stick, it is those within me who do so, and the stick I produce is the last link in an immemorial stick tradition. All the stick producers before me and all the sticks they produced are somehow here with me now. Although they are dead and decayed, they are immortal. And I will be, too, and the stick I produce, if I pass it along to the next stick producer. To become immortal, however, to be remembered, my stick must be slightly different from all previous sticks (slightly more beautiful or functional), so that it (and myself) will not be confused with previous stick productions. Thus, the production of sticks is a challenge to overcome death and become immortal. To put it less selfishly: it is a challenge to live for others and live on with them. If the stick I produce makes me immortal, though, and gives my life meaning and surpasses death, how do I avoid forgetting the original purpose of stick production, which was to open a pathway in the forest? § In this effort to untangle the Gordian knot binding us to cultural objects, and which makes us subject to them, an important aspect of history comes to the fore: culture, originally a method for liberating man from natural conditions, has become an end in itself — such that the purpose of culture is forgotten. In fact, if we look at the culture surrounding us, all these enormously complex works of technology and art, and the equally complex immaterial structures sustaining them, we are impressed by the amount of accumulated knowledge, creative imagination, and existential commitment standing behind culture, and we take for granted the fact that it failed in its purpose to deliver us from objective conditions. All our efforts to change cultural conditions — all political and aesthetic revolutions and reforms — are aimed at the way the arts and technological gadgets are used and not at the contradiction presented by these gadgets. We have forgotten that, if we want to be free, we must try to overcome the intrinsic contradiction of sticks, not make increasingly better sticks or have them manipulated by increasingly better people.

§ Something unexpected is happening, though, which, if it were not actually happening, would strike us as utterly fantastic. The Gordian knot binding us to objects and which makes us subject to them, is being cut, and it is being cut by the very art and technology that knotted it in the first place. This has a deceptively simple name: "automation." To understand the ramifications of this takes some effort.

§ This article has offered the following version of history and the present situation: man, this alienated being who dwells between what is and what should be, attempts to change that which is into that which should be, in order to liberate himself from objective conditions. In this attempt, he becomes increasingly enmeshed with objects, so that now, at the end of history, he is even more conditioned — although on a different level. It now appears that this human attempt to inject values into phenomena (at producing culture) consists of two distinct phases. In the first phase, values were chosen and phenomena were examined with a view toward these values. In the second phase, the values were actually embedded in phenomena, or phenomena were forced onto values. For instance, in the first phase, I would like to have a stick when entering a forest and I know that branches are good for stick making. In the second phase, I force the stick to become a branch. No doubt these two phases implicate one another in the complex Gordian-knot pattern discussed earlier; but they are still two distinct phases. It now happens that the first phase (hereafter called "programming"), may be neatly separated from the second phase (previously "work" and hereafter "automation"). This separation shows that the gesture forcing phenomena to become values (the gesture previously called "work") is, in fact, not a human gesture at all, but something occurring entirely within the phenomenal world. What is human is the first phase, and the first phase only. § The common-sense conclusion drawn from this is that to work is a gesture unworthy of man, that it must be relegated to automatic machines so that man may concentrate exclusively on programming and the world may become automated, as it should be. But this is a hasty conclusion. What the neat distinction between programming and actual work suggests is that we must return our attention to the values from which we were distracted by the perfidious resistance in the inertia of the phenomena on which we worked. The important feature of automation is not that it delivers us from that perfidious resistance (machines have to bear it now), but it challenges us to face values. For instance, if I no longer need to tear a branch off a tree and turn it into a stick because a robot does this for me, why should I program the robot to make a stick — particularly if it is the robot and not me going into the forest? § In this situation (which undoubtedly foreshadows our own), there is no longer talk of an "inner contradiction within sticks," or an "internal dialectics within modes of production." Man is no longer involved with sticks and stick making; he is no longer subject to objects. In fact, he is no longer a subject in any meaningful sense of that term. All the fascinating and inebriating aspects of the Gordian knot discussed earlier in this paper have been overcome, and this may be called "unconditional freedom." Technology and all the other arts will overcome their intrinsic contradictions, almost without our noticing, and set us free from objective conditions. At a price, however: what is so frivolously called "the price of freedom." § The price of freedom is that we have to turn our attention to values. We have to ask ourselves, "What ought to be?" "What do we want?" "Why are we programming robots?" "What good is our newly won freedom?" From the beginning, man has negated that which is, because it is not as it should be; this was called "spirit." Now we must decide how the world should be, and this is called "freedom." Man must now turn himself around, just as he turned branches around. Instead of advancing into what is, we must advance into values. Our question is no longer "Freedom from what?" but "Freedom, what for?" We have not yet begun to answer that question. We are, as far as values are concerned, in the Lower Palaeolithic Era. § Of course, this appears to be utter nonsense. Everyone knows what he wants, what should be. For instance, everyone wants to eat, make love, be in good health, and live long — forever, if possible. By extension, we want everyone else to have this, too. But these are not really values; they are only means of attaining values. They are tools with which we do something. Automation will provide us with these tools, sooner or later (preferably later than sooner). It is the ends of these means, and which give meaning, which are under question. Why do I want to eat, other than to digest and eat more? This question, which we must face for the first time (although continually formulated, it was never a serious question until now), shows that we are no longer interested in changing the world, but in giving meaning to changing the world. § From the beginning, humans have been subject to objects. It is now possible to envision that this will no longer be the case. It sounds like paradise: everything that should be, will be; everything we want will be at our disposal. However, it may be more like hell: not knowing what we want, humans may be plunged back into the abyss from which we have been saved thus far by our struggle with objects. Unless, of course, some heretofore unthinkable method can be found to choose values. After all, isn't this the business of art, once it is freed from contradiction, once it no longer has to battle objects and can concentrate solely on meaning? *

ADDITIONAL IMAGE INFORMATION

§ *Fractal Pleasure* (1989), Dan Sandin, Ellen Sandor & Stephan Meyers, (art) n: Reproduced with Vivian Sobchack's "A Theory of Everything: Meditations on Total Chaos," *Artforum* (October 1990): 151. Flusser's "On Popes" appeared in the same issue. § *Fourplay* (1990), John Hart, Ellen Sandor & Stephan Meyers, (art) n: Reproduced with Vivian Sobchack's "A Theory of Everything: Meditations on Total Chaos," *Artforum* (October 1990). § *Aspects of Gaia* (1989), Roy Ascott: Flusser participated in an Ars Electronica symposium in 1988 with Jean Baudrillard, Hannes Böhringer, Heinz von Foerster, Friedrich Kittler and Peter Weibel, published as the book *Philosophien der neuen Technologie* (Berlin, Merve Verlag, 1989). § *Organe et Fonction d'Alice au Pays des Merveilles* (1985), Roy Ascott: Flusser saw the exhibition "Les Immatériaux" (1985) at the Centre Georges Pompidou in Paris, organized by Jean-François Lyotard and Thierry Chaput, director of the Centre de Création Industrielle. The exhibition impacted

Flusser's thinking about technical images and he cited it in "The Photograph as Post-Industrial Object: An Essay on the Ontological Standing of Photographs," *Leonardo*, Vol. 19, No. 4 (1986): 329-332. § *Five Into One* (1991), Matt Mullican: An image of a model utopian city made with a supercomputer designed by artificial intelligence researchers, from Mullican's *Connection Machine-2* (1989) installation, exhibited at the Museum of Modern Art in New York in 1989 and reviewed in *Artforum* (January 1990): 141-42. An image of a wool rug designed by Mullican, *Untitled* (1989), was used to illustrate Flusser's "On an Unspeakable Future," *Artforum* (March 1990): 22. § *Into the Rainbow* (1983), Dieter Jung: Holograms were one of Flusser's favorite examples of technical images and he mentioned them frequently in his writings. § *Architectural Site 8* (1986), Barbara Kasten: Reproduced alongside a review of Kasten's exhibition at the International Center of Photography in New York, *Artforum* (December 1989): 138. § *The Electronic Bible and the Persian Gulf War* (1991), Fred Forest: Flusser collaborated with Forest on the video "The Gestures of the Professor" (1972) and other projects relating to video, phenomenology, and gestures. § *The Illuminated Man* (1969), Duane Michals: Used to illustrate Flusser's "On Discovery II," *Artforum* (October 1987): 12. § *Lavandula Angustifolia* (1984), Joan Fontcuberta: From Fontcuberta's *Herbarium* series of imaginary plants. Flusser and Fontcuberta were both interested in the intersection of art, science, and images. Fontcuberta wrote about Flusser's philosophy of photography, primarily in relation to his own work, and Flusser wrote an introduction to Fontcuberta's book *Herbarium* (1985). § *Evolution II: Chimpanzee and Man* (1984), Nancy Burson: Reproduced alongside Flusser's "Reflections: Nancy Burson: Chimeras," *European Photography* (January 1988): 46. Flusser wrote that Burson's photographs were "chimeras" of a new world: fabulous beasts, like the Chimera in ancient Greece, except created out of pixels and serving as models for future genetic manipulations. § *GFP Bunny* (2000), Eduardo Kac: Coinciding with ideas outlined in the "Curie's Children" column,

the *GFP Bunny* was made with the assistance of Louis Bec, Flusser's collaborator on the parabiological text *Vampyroteuthis infernalis: A Treatise with a Report by the Institute Scientifique de Recherche Paranaturaliste* (1987). § *Sign System for Electro Medical Instruments* (1964), Tomas Maldonado and Gui Bonsiepe: Reproduced alongside Flusser's "On an Unspeakable Future," *Artforum* (March 1990): 22.
§ *Le mie parole (My Words)* (1973), Ketty La Rocca: An exhibition of La Rocca's work appeared at Galleria Carini in Florence, Italy and was reviewed in *Artforum* (March 1990): 171. La Rocca's combination of language, gestures, and photography overlaps with Flusser's philosophy, interest in concrete poetry, and his posthumously published book *Gestures* (1991).
§ *1117; Geysers and how they are explained* (1986), Andrew Masullo: Photograph of a detail of Masullo's painting published alongside Flusser's "On Books," *Artforum* (November 1991): 15. § *Untitled (No Radio)* (1988), Barbara Kruger: Published with Carol Squiers's column "Special Effects" ("On Photo Allure"), *Artforum* (December 1990): 19. Kruger wrote a column on

television for *Artforum*, "Remote Control" (1985-90), that ran alongside Flusser's "Curie's Children." § *Green Mask* (1986), Sarah Charlesworth: An image from "A Grammar of Essence," an *Artforum* (February 1990) project that connected ancient technology, ritual, and representation and paralleled Flusser's arguments in *Towards a Philosophy of Photography* (1983). § *Rosetta Stone, Channel 10* (1983), Nam June Paik. Flusser and Paik participated in "Open Circuits: The Future of Television" (1974), a symposium at the Museum of Modern Art in New York, and their paths crossed periodically throughout their careers. § *Deyrolle Taxidermy, Paris* (1986), Richard Ross: Used to illustrate Daniel Soutif's "Pictures and an Exhibition" essay on museums and photography, *Artforum* (March 1991): 83-89. § Institut du Monde Arabe, Paris (1987), Jean Nouvel, Pierre Soria, Gilbert Lézénès, and Architecture Studio (Martin Robain, Jean-François Galmiche, Rodo Tisnado, and Jean-François Bonne); Photo, Georges Fessy: Reproduced in Mario Pisani's "Body Building," about the division between "Postmodern" and "Neo-Modern" factions in contemporary architecture, *Artforum* (April 1988): 101-107. The article appeared in the same issue as Flusser's "On Discovery IV." § *Tourisms: suitCase Studies* (1991), Elizabeth Diller and Ricardo Scofidio: Reproduced alongside a review of their exhibition at M.I.T. List Visual Arts Center, *Artforum* (November 1991): 140. § *Deutsches Museum München I* (1990), Candida Höfer: Reproduced in Daniel Soutif's "Pictures and an Exhibition." § *Total Recall* (1987), Gretchen Bender: Bender asked Flusser to participate in a 1992 symposium at the Dia Center for the Arts in New York, arranged with Timothy Druckrey, that resulted in the book *Culture on the Brink: Ideologies of Technology* (Seattle: Bay Press, 1994). Flusser agreed to participate, but he died in a car accident in November 1991. § *Tree Trunk with Broken Bungalow and Shotgun Houses* (1989), James Casebere: Reproduced alongside a review of Casebere's exhibition at Vrej Baghoomian Gallery in New York, *Artforum* (May 1990): 186. Flusser's "On Future Architecture" appeared in the same issue. § *Koyaanisqatsi* (1983), Godfrey Reggio: Reproduced alongside Flusser's "On Discovery," *Artforum* (March

1988): 14-15. § *Catchphrases-Catchimages: A Conversation with Vilém Flusser* (1986), Harun Farocki. § *Karlsruhe, Siemens* (1991), Andreas Gursky: Reproduced with a review of Gursky's exhibition at 303 Gallery in New York, *Artforum* (December 1991): 101. § *The Brooklyn Bridge, Nov. 28ᵗʰ* (1982), David Hockney: Reproduced alongside Flusser's "On Popes," *Artforum* (October 1990): 26. § *Evocation of Faust: Charming Landscape* (1987), Dara Birnbaum: From Birnbaum's *Out of the Blue* project for *Artforum* (March 1988) that appeared in the same issue as Flusser's "On Discovery III." § *Los Angeles Airport* (1978-83), Garry Winogrand: Reproduced alongside Flusser's "On Discovery IV," *Artforum* (April 1988): 14. § *Reach (Phantom Limb Series) (1986)*, Lynn Hershman Leeson: Leeson's exhibition at the Collective for Living Cinema in New York was reviewed in *Artforum* (Summer 1989), the same issue as Flusser's "Wondering About Science." § *Untitled (Meeting With Venus de Milo Series)* (1991), Lizzie Calligas: Flusser wrote about Calligas's work in *European Photography* and for her exhibition catalogue *Metamorphosis: My body-your body* (Athens: Ileana Tounta, 1990).

Additional Image Information

† This book was composed by Chagrin using Jenson Recut and Montserrat fonts.

© 2017 Metaflux Publishing, UK

www.metafluxpublishing.com

ISBN 978 0 9933272 3 0